Nothing Better Than This

ALSO AVAILABLE
BY EUGENE W. BAKER

A Noble Example: A Pen Picture of William M. Tryon, Pioneer Texas Baptist Preacher and Co-Founder of Baylor University

In His Traces: The Life and Times of R. E. B. Baylor

Nothing Better Than This

The Biography of James Huckins,
First Baptist Missionary to Texas

Eugene W. Baker

BIG BEAR BOOKS

Originally published in 1985 by Baylor University Press, Waco, Texas 76798

All Rights Reserved
Library of Congress Catalog Card Number: 85-70395
ISBN: 0-933335-00-8

New paperback ISBN: 978-1-60258-580-5

Printed in the United States of America

In honor of my brother, John Thomas Baker,
and in memory of my brother, Robert Erin Baker

Foreword

Eugene Baker has made an immeasurable contribution to our knowledge of and appreciation for the work of our early Baptist fathers in Texas.

The first sermon ever preached in the brisk and bustling little village at Allen's Landing on the banks of Buffalo Bayou in what was to become Houston, Texas, was delivered by the pioneer Baptist preacher Z. N. Morrell. Little did anyone ever dream on that auspicious spring morning that a century and a half later Houston would become the home of the largest association of Baptists in the world.

Barely two years after the Reverend Morrell's sermon, two missionaries, William M. Tryon and James Huckins, were sent to Texas by the American Baptist Home Mission Society headquartered in New York. Tryon went to Independence to begin his work, and Huckins, among his varied responsibilities, became the first pastor of the First Baptist Church in Houston on April 10, 1841. Chartered with 19 white members and 4 black members and living on a salary of $400 a year, the noble pastor and visionary people began a work upon which has grown not only a noble and mighty church 146 years later, but a ministry that was destined to have far-reaching effects in the Southern Baptist denomination in Texas. Evangelism, education, ministry—all the things that make Texas great today, have roots that go deep into the soil of Pastor Huckins's heart.

Lest we forget how far we have come and who has planted and watered before us, we do well from time to time to pause and reflect in order that appreciation might be expressed to man and glory given to God. The First Baptist church of Houston and her 18,000 members owe no small debt to Pastor Huckins and his fledgling congregation, and it is one that we greatly acknowledge and for which we gratefully pray.

Today at the heart of Houston there stands a great church with a people whose hearts beat as one with the glory of our Lord and of His kingdom and for the evangelization of the lost world. Over 125 students have gone into the seminary, over 75 million dollars have been given to the Lord's work, and approximately 12,000 have been won to Christ in the last decade and a half alone. All of this was made possible because of the commitment and sacrifice of those who have gone before. Traced to its ultimate source, there stands the name of James Huckins and 23 brave and faithful souls whose names are known only to God who planted our beloved First Baptist Church of Houston on the Rock of Ages Himself. Referring to His own deity, Jesus said, "Upon this rock I will build my church." As lively stones, it has been our grateful privilege to build upon Him who is the living stone for more than a century on the work that has gone before . . . the preaching of Pastor Huckins and the faithfulness of God's people. Our forefathers have continued to build our church and so shall we greatly continue to do until our Lord's glorious return.

John Bisagno
Pastor, First Baptist Church
Houston, Texas

Preface

This book provides a chronological view of the life of James Huckins (1807–1863). It is a look at the man and his accomplishments, seen through his deep commitment to Christian service.

Records are practically nonexistent on his early life and are scant on his activities prior to his appointment as a missionary to Texas in 1839. For the next two decades his life was richly interwoven with the creation and early development of the Galveston Baptist Church, Houston Baptist Church, Union Baptist Association, Baptist State Convention, Baylor University, and the Howard Association of Galveston. There is more material available on this period, but often the names and places are unclear. The last few years of his life were a blur of fatigue as he ministered untiringly in Charleston, South Carolina, to help those who suffered the wreckage of the Civil War. A few letters, newspaper reports, and denominational minutes provide the basic information on this traumatic period.

Although Huckins appears to be a paragon of virtue, there are some facets of his life that indicate otherwise, at least in the eyes of a few people. His forced resignation from the pastorate of the Galveston Baptist Church in 1847, shortly after completing a year-long fund-raising effort and building program for the congregation, is difficult to understand. The deacons requested him to leave because of prejudices held by some of the members. Extensive research has failed to reveal details of the circumstances surrounding this event.

Huckins continued to love the church. When he returned to its pastorate five years later, nothing appears to indicate bitterness on the part of himself or any of the members, except one who disliked Huckins because of his apparent mistreatment of a household slave some years before. However, the congregation voted down this individual's request for Huckins's censure in January 1859. The spirit of the church appeared to be harmonious during the entire time of Huckins's second term as its minister.

The decision of Huckins in the fall of 1859 to leave Galveston and accept a pastorate in Charleston, South Carolina, might have been caused by the failure of the Galveston church to grow in numbers or by discontent over Huckins's devotion to the activities of the Howard Association. Any attempt to prove this, however, would be mere speculation and would not take into account the probable "call" of God.

Huckins may have harbored some ill feelings for the Galveston congregation as perhaps indicated in a letter to the editor of the *South Western Baptist* of Alabama in the summer of 1860. In that letter he corrects the publisher's account of a gift given Huckins by the Galveston community, but no evidence exists to show that he did so out of any bitterness toward the Galveston church members. In fact, all evidence points to Huckins's love for those people. His notification to the editor that no Baptist, "directly or indirectly," had any part in the surprise gift may have been only an attempt to identify properly the contributors in an effort to show the extent of the love held for him throughout Galveston. It is unfortunate that more evidence is not available to provide additional insight into Huckins's motivations.

In spite of these unexplained inconsistencies, the story of James Huckins is a remarkable account of an individual devoted to the cause of Christ. To present it adequately would require virtually every color on an artist's palette and every typeface in a printer's tray to enliven the vignettes that contribute to the totality of his life.

He was an orphan, scholar, preacher, pastor, husband, father, counselor, evangelist, church organizer, administrator, businessman, educator, fund-raiser, slave owner, community leader, missionary, and Confederate Army chaplain. He was all these things and more—but most of all he was just an ordinary individual who had an extraordinary purpose in life—to serve Jesus Christ, no matter where he had to go or what he had to do.

To James Huckins, there was nothing better than this.

e.w.b.

Acknowledgments

Many individuals provided valuable assistance in the research and preparation of this volume. Notable among them are Mr. Kent Keeth, director, and Mrs. Ellen Brown, archivist, The Texas Collection, Baylor University, Waco, Texas; Mr. Ben Rogers, archivist, The Southwestern Baptist Theological Seminary, Fort Worth, Texas; Ms. Jane Kenamore, archivist, The Rosenberg Library, Galveston, Texas; Ms. Susan Eltscher, assistant archivist, American Baptist Historical Society, Rochester, New York; and Mrs. Elizabeth Wills, special collections librarian, Samford University, Birmingham, Alabama.

The author also is extremely grateful for the materials supplied by the library staffs of Furman University, Mercer University, Yale University, Harvard University, Brown University, University of Alabama, Baylor University, Louisiana State University, Andover-Newton Theological School, Southwestern Baptist Theological Seminary, and the Dargan-Carver Library in Nashville, Tennessee, as well as staff members of the state libraries of New York, New Hampshire, Vermont, Massachusetts, South Carolina, Georgia, Alabama, and Texas. In addition, the services provided by research librarians in the Library of Congress, and the public libraries in New York City; Waco, Texas; Savannah, Georgia; New Haven, Connecticut; Boston, Massachusetts; Concord, New Hampshire; Providence, Rhode Island; and Memphis, Tennessee are deeply appreciated.

A special word of gratitude goes to Dr. Herbert H. Reynolds, president, Baylor University, for providing the insight, direction, and opportunity to engage in this endeavor.

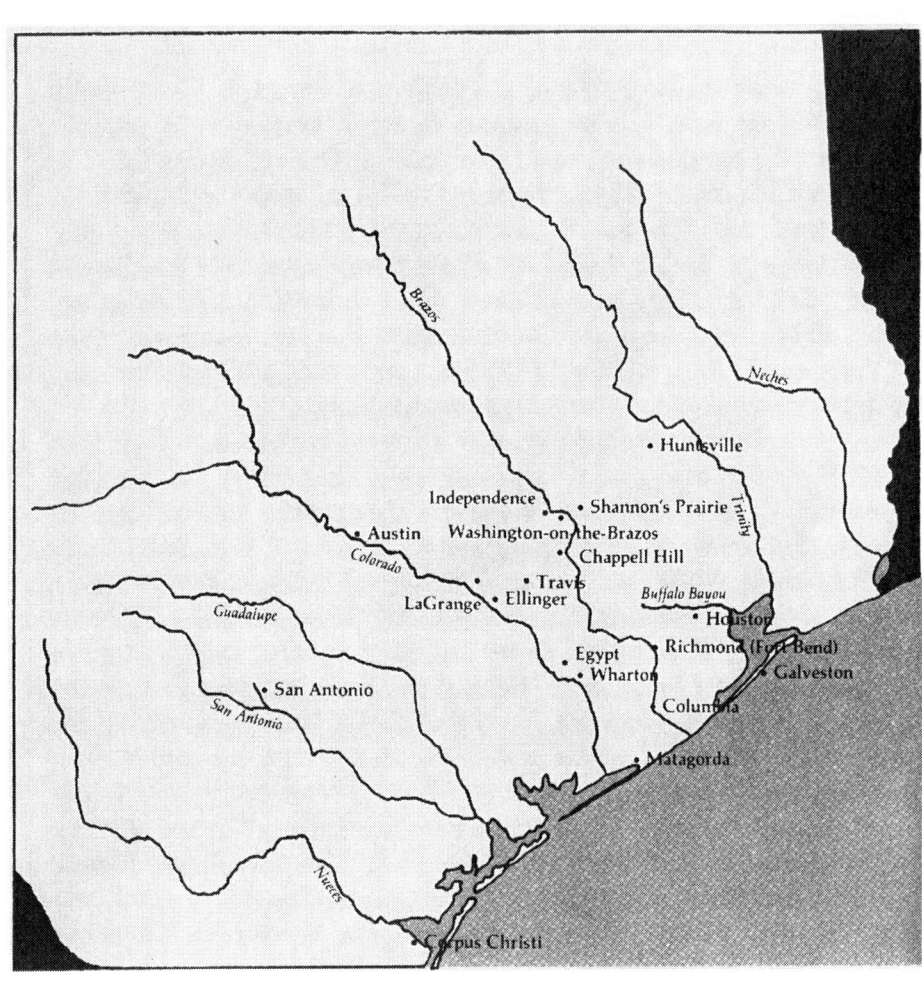

1

ON 8 APRIL 1807, a boy was born into a small home in Dorchester, a tiny village nestled in the rolling green hills of central New Hampshire. The father, James Huckins, a carpenter by trade, was well known in the community and made a comfortable living. He gave his infant son his own name and hoped he would grow up and follow in his footsteps. Filling his father's shoes would have been a respectable future for this lad, now the seventh generation of the Huckins clan in America.[1] And the young boy might have done so, but the death of his father and mother during a spotted fever epidemic in 1813 dramatically eliminated that opportunity. James, only six years old, and his sister, Mary, two years younger, were suddenly orphans and alone; all plans for his future evaporated.

James faced additional trauma when he and Mary were separated shortly after their parents' deaths and taken in by different families. Mary was placed in the home of a local physician, and James moved in with a wealthy farmer and his wife who had no children and wanted to make James their legitimate heir. A farm, cattle, and money—a very good second chance in life. James forfeited that bright prospect, however, a few years later when he decided to become a Christian.

At fourteen, his commitment to Christ was extremely mature. Frequently he spent afternoons in the woods near his house praying and communing with the Lord, gradually deciding to devote his life completely to his new master by becoming a minister. Huckins's preoccupation with religion greatly displeased his "adopted" parents, and his choice of vocation eventually led to his expulsion from their home.[2]

Though only a young teenager, and still a neophyte Christian, Huckins undauntedly clung to his calling, constantly praying that God would open a way for him to obtain the education necessary for his ministerial preparation. His earnestness and perseverance touched the heart of Abner Forbes, a former Vermont militia general and prominent New England Baptist.[3]

Forbes served as the treasurer of the Union Society of Vermont and New Hampshire, a missionary and education society, and was an active leader of the Woodstock Baptist Association, an organization of several churches in New Hampshire and Vermont. He took a personal interest in Huckins and arranged for him to pursue his education in New Hampton, a small town in the White Mountain foothills of central New Hampshire where the Baptists of that state operated the New Hampton Academical and Theological Institution.[4]

Begun in 1821 as a private endeavor, the academy was housed in a two-story frame building on the town common and was heated by an open fireplace. It had no library, scientific equipment, or even blackboards. The pine desks and seats were plain and unpainted. The surrounding community generally entertained the notion that education spoiled children for work and that learning was an aristocratic luxury. However, in spite of these drawbacks, the school was fairly successful in attracting students. When Huckins entered in 1826, the institution had students enrolled from every New England state.[5] His expenses at the school were met by funds from the Massachusetts Baptist Education Society, in which General Forbes was a prominent leader.[6]

The curriculum at the New Hampton Academical and Theological Institution included studies in geography, geometry, English, history, philosophy, chemistry, Greek, Latin, and political economy. All students were required to participate in daily devotional activities and to attend public worship on Sundays. A rhetorical exercise, held every week, consisted of declamations, dissertations, written and extemporaneous debates, and special lessons in reading.[7]

These activities whetted Huckins's academic and religious appetites and initiated his lifelong passion for knowledge and spiritual insight. One evidence of his interest in scholarly pursuits was his involvement in the founding of the Literary Adelphi during his second year at the institution. The organization was designed to encourage students to develop their minds, to acquire useful knowledge, and to improve communicative skills.[8]

After two years at New Hampton, Huckins moved to Providence, Rhode Island, a two-century-old city situated at the head of the tidewater of Narragansett Bay, thirty miles from the Atlantic Ocean. Providence had a population of more than twenty thousand and was one of the leading manufacturing and seaport cities in New England.[9]

There Huckins enrolled in the preparatory school of Brown University, an adjunct program of the institution's educational system.[10] The university, originally called Rhode Island College, had approximately two hundred students enrolled in 1828. That was its sixty-fourth year of existence but only its fifty-eighth year of operation, since it had disbanded for about five years during the American Revolutionary War.[11]

The government of the university was vested in a twelve-member Board of Fellows, eight of whom, including the president, were required to be Baptist, and a Board of Trustees, of whom twenty-two of the thirty-six had to belong to the Baptist faith. The president was Dr. Francis Wayland, former pastor of the First Baptist Church of Boston, who had assumed leadership of the university in December 1826.[12]

In the fall of 1828 Huckins became a student at the university and moved into Hope College, a four-story edifice that served as a dormitory and also housed several offices. The only other building on campus—University Hall—also contained dormitory rooms and offices as well as the chapel, library, and museum.[13]

A very serious student, Huckins devoted such close attention to his studies that he caused serious injury to his eyesight, already poor because of lack of muscle control in one of his eyes.[14] Nevertheless, he continually sought opportunities to read and to learn. With that aim in mind, he joined the Philermenian Society during his second year. The primary purposes of this select forty-five-member group were the acquisition of knowledge, the interchange of ideas, and the development of literary skills. Huckins was very active in all the endeavors of this society.

In his senior year Huckins became engaged to Rhoda Barton, a descendant of John Alden of the *Mayflower* and granddaughter of Revolutionary War hero General William Barton. In July 1777 Barton, then a lieutenant colonel, had led a forty-one-man group in a daring night raid into the headquarters of British Major General Richard Prescot and captured him. For this extraordinary feat he was honored by the United States Congress with a specially engraved gold and silver sword.[15]

Rhoda, a highly cultured young lady and an accomplished poet, was a native of East Windsor, Connecticut. She attended the historic First Baptist Church of Providence, where she and her parents, John and Hannah West Barton, were members.[16] This church, the oldest Baptist church in America, had been established in 1639 by Roger Williams shortly after his escape from Massachusetts to avoid religious persecution.

James married Rhoda on 18 September 1832, shortly after his graduation from Brown University. Three days later he was ordained by the First Baptist Church in South Reading, Massachusetts, which had called him to become its fourth pastor.[17] Located about ten miles northeast of Boston, the town was originally a part of Reading, a four-mile-square area that had been purchased from the Indians in 1640. It had separated from Reading in 1812 to form a distinct municipality. Through the years it had grown to fifteen hundred residents and had become a manufacturing center, chiefly of women's shoes.[18]

The congregation of the South Reading church was typical of

the Baptist churches in Massachusetts that had been steadily increasing in number since the 1660s, primarily because of the denomination's evangelistic and missionary zeal. In 1802 the Baptists of the state established a Missionary Society to support a program of mission work in the Northeast and in several Pacific Islands. That society spawned an unusual interest in education among Baptists that led to the formation of several educational organizations.[19]

In 1818, when the First Baptist church of South Reading was but fourteen years old, the congregation organized the first Sunday school in the town and ten years later founded an academy to prepare young men for college and for the ministry. In 1830 the church sent out its first missionary, who served among the Western Indians.

For two years immediately prior to Huckins's arrival in the fall of 1832, John Pratt, principal of the academy, had filled the pulpit of the church. Even though officially not the pastor, he served effectively, raising the membership to more than 125, including approximately 40 whom he baptized in 1831.[20]

Huckins eagerly entered his first pastorate and soon experienced success similar to Reverend Pratt's, baptizing more than thirty members into the church.[21] However, after only eight months, he accepted the pastorate of the First Baptist Church of Andover, Massachusetts, and moved to the town in May 1833. The church had been organized in September 1832, on the day of Huckins's ordination, and had not had a pastor until his arrival.[22]

Located about twenty miles north of Boston, Andover was the largest township in Essex County, with over thirty-five thousand acres and nearly four thousand people. A manufacturing center with several woolen mills, the town was the home of Andover Theological Seminary, founded in 1807, and of Phillips Academy, established in 1778 and one of the first preparatory schools for boys in the country.[23]

At Andover Huckins had many responsibilities besides preaching. He had been there only a month when the church added to his pastoral duties the responsibilities of clerk. That winter he became a fund-raiser when he was called upon to canvass the community for contributions to build a new church, for which he was named construction superintendent. Huckins gave one hundred dollars to the campaign.[24] Nicolas Brown of Providence, namesake of Huckins's alma mater, was among the largest contributors.[25]

For the next several months Huckins labored arduously in an attempt to meet the spiritual needs of the congregation as well as to administer the church operations, raise funds, and direct all construction activities. Though extremely time-consuming and physically taxing, these tasks provided Huckins valuable experience that would prove advantageous to him in his future ministry.

After two and a half years at Andover, Huckins accepted the challenge of a new opportunity in Calais, Maine, a progressive community on the southwest bank of the St. Croix River, the border between the United States and Canada. At the turn of the nineteenth century Calais had numbered less than a hundred inhabitants, but the richness of its soil and the commercial potential of its harbors had gradually attracted more settlers into the area.

One of the major interests of the citizens of Calais was education. In fact, the majority of the town's early tax levy was for the support of its schools.[26] The townsfolk, however, displayed less interest in developing religious organizations. When Maine became a state in 1820 Calais had about four hundred inhabitants, but there were no churches of any kind in the community. The widely separated pioneers in the area did meet occasionally for worship, but no ministers participated in these activities. During the first five years of statehood, the population of Calais more than quadrupled, and in 1825 a Congregational church was organized in the "thrifty cultured town."[27] Seven years later, primarily as the result of a revival movement sparked by the preaching of a Baptist evangelist, the First Baptist Church was established with eleven members. After only three months, the membership had so increased that forty individuals left and started another church across the river in St. Stephen, Canada. Within a year, both congregations had grown substantially and each had its own meeting house.

The major emphasis of the First Baptist Church in Calais

during its formative years had been the dissemination of the Gospel to "awaken an interest in religion wherever a hearing could be obtained."[28] The congregation had frequently sponsored religious meetings throughout eastern Maine, and had added greatly to the Baptist influence in the state. The evangelistic fervor was still very much prevalent when Huckins arrived in Calais in October 1835 with his wife and two-year-old daughter, Caroline, to become the church's third pastor.[29] Under his leadership the evangelistic spirit continued to flourish, and church membership grew to one hundred thirty-seven within a year, sixty of the new members being children whom Huckins baptized.[30]

During the next two years both James Huckins and his wife were not only active in their church, but also in community organizations, principally the Ladies Benevolent Society of Milltown, a village on the outskirts of Calais. The society had been formed in 1828 to assist the suffering "regardless of sect or nationality," but had been dormant for several years before the leadership of Huckins and his wife revived its work.[31]

That experience in community service would be invaluable to Huckins in the years ahead. But, perhaps, another experience that occurred in the winter of 1838 would prove even more valuable, enabling him to be able to empathize with many to whom he would minister in the future. During the extremely cold months of February and March, Huckins was seriously ill and had to be nursed day and night by his wife. Caring for him drained her physical stamina, and one evening, after a particularly exhausting day, she left his room and took their two-year-old daughter, Emeline, in her arms to seek rest in another room. Although Rhoda's energies were restored by sleep in the unheated room, extreme cold caused the child to become sick. While weakened, Emeline developed scarlet fever and died on 24 March.[32]

Emeline's death drew the members of the church close together spiritually, and for the next several weeks they worked harmoniously to such an extent that many new members were added and a mission was started.[33] That summer, however, religious enthusiasm was disturbed by the arrival in Calais of Ichabod

Codding, an abolitionist lecturer. He had been sent by General Samuel Fessenden, a prominent lawyer, staunch abolitionist, and ardent disciple of William Lloyd Garrison. Some of the town's political leaders, concerned that Codding's comments might cause unrest, opposed his speaking in the Town Hall. Because of that opposition, Codding turned to James Huckins and the members of the First Baptist Church, asking for permission to hold his lectures in their sanctuary.

This was not Huckins's first experience with abolitionists or antislavery sentiment, for he had been exposed to both on several occasions. While a student at Brown University, he had heard the slavery issue frequently discussed by President Francis Wayland, an outspoken opponent of its evils.[34] During his first pastorate at South Reading, two antislavery societies had been established in the Reading area, one of which was the first female antislavery organization ever formed in America.[35] The Salem Baptist Association, to which Huckins's church in South Reading and also in Andover, had belonged, had advocated principles congruent with the abolitionist philosophy since 1831.[36]

The issue of slavery, of course, had been a major topic of conversation for Americans since black people were first brought into the country, and more especially as the United States developed its constitution. The ensuing years had served to broaden the bases of support for those who favored and for those who opposed the institution. In the early 1830s, with significant increases in the number of antislavery societies and an outpouring of literature against such involuntary servitude, a variety of organizations had become actively involved, with discussions generally taking on a northern antislavery or a southern proslavery bias.

Most church groups, especially Baptists, attempted to abstain from any formal policy favoring either position, preferring to avoid controversy and feeling that it was not in their best interests to make an issue of the subject. Gradually, however, some religious bodies boldly began to denounce slavery, and these denunciations soon were countered by equally pious pronouncements from other religious groups in support of the system.[37] New England became a seedbed for abolitionist organizations, although not all groups agreed on means or methods of operation. Many Baptists in those states, inspired by the Baptist involvement in the successful British emancipation movement, formed antislavery groups and began to publicly proclaim their opinions. This led to the formation of similar societies by likeminded enthusiasts in several southern states.[38]

Toward the end of the 1830s many state and national antislavery organizations began having major administrative and financial problems, but still many individuals and religious groups remained actively engaged in propagandizing for emancipation.[39] One of these groups was Maine's Washington Baptist Association with which the First Baptist Church of Calais was associated. The association was formed in 1835 when the Eastern Maine Association had divided to form the Hancock and the Washington Associations.[40] In 1837 that body officially resolved to refrain from fellowship with those individuals who advocated or practiced slavery.[41]

Not all members of the association, however, were abolitionists, and many disagreed with this policy. One of them was T. J. D. Hadley, a town officer of Calais and member of the First Baptist Church. In the summer of 1838, when Ichabod Codding made his request to deliver antislavery messages in the church, Hadley and a few of his friends vigorously opposed granting permission. Others, however, were in favor, and dissension soon arose among the congregation's 125 members. Huckins sided with the proslavery clique and refused the request, but Samuel Kelly, a deacon in the church who controlled more than half the pews, felt the people of the town should have the opportunity to hear Codding. Overruling his pastor, he opened the church "even at the risk of its being torn down or burned by a mob." The lectures were delivered at the church without incident, but when Codding attempted to repeat his discussions the next week in the Town Hall, he was pelted with rotten eggs and driven out of Calais.[42]

Shortly after these incidents the abolitionist movement began to gain popularity in Calais. The position which Huckins had taken in the abolitionist lecturer controversy was well known and caused unrest in both the church and the town. As a result of the potential injury to his ministry, Huckins resigned his pastorate in September, receiving a letter of recommendation from the church "to any Society that might desire his services."[43] He then went to Providence to join his wife, who, earlier that summer, had moved to her parents' home where she had given birth to their third child, Sarah, on 22 August 1838.

A few weeks later, Huckins accepted a commission from the American Baptist Home Mission Society headquartered in New York. Baptists had been involved in foreign mission activities since 1814 when the General Convention of the Baptist Denomination of the United States for Foreign Missions was organized. Although mission work in the various states and territories was conducted under the auspices of this body, "home" missions were not officially established until 1832 when the Home Mission Society was formed to promote mission programs in North America.

In its first year of operation, the Home Mission Society employed fifty missionaries in twelve states, though only four of them were assigned to the South. During the next several years, however, the society made numerous appointments to the southern states. Huckins's commission in November 1838 called for him to raise funds in Georgia and South Carolina. Knowing that his travel schedule would leave little time to be with his family, he left them in Providence and set out for his new field of labor. It was the first of many long separations from his family that he would be called upon to make in his service for Christ.

HIS WAS AN ARDUOUS TASK and a very lonely one at times, but he was dedicated to his calling. He traveled from place to place by stagecoach, by horseback, and sometimes by boat, preaching five or six times a week, with up to fifty and sixty miles between appointments.[44] The size of the town and the distance he had to travel did not matter to him; he wanted only to share the story of the work of the Home Mission Society with as many as would listen. He especially enjoyed "talking about the love of Christ" with other ministers, as he felt this helped restore his spirits.[45]

He eagerly looked forward to letters from his wife, and when he failed to receive one as expected he became depressed. When he arrived in Savannah, Georgia, on 14 December 1838 and did not have a letter waiting from his wife, his heart was "ready to sink." Feeling, however, that she had not neglected him but rather that "God has ordered it thus to try my faith," he did not complain.[46]

During the last week of December while still in Savannah, Huckins wrote to his wife describing his activities and his "painful loneliness." He missed her greatly and told her he would be willing to walk forty miles in the rain if only he could be with her and their children for one hour. "But the cause of Christ demands the sacrifice," he added, "and I am probably doing more good than I was ever doing."[47]

Although Huckins was unhappy away from his family, he was pleased to be in the South during the winter months. In the same letter he wrote, "I do not believe I should have lived this winter if I had stayed at the north. I am confident my lungs would have become diseased. The hand of God I believe has been with me." He also urged Rhoda to draw closer to the Cross and "be willing like him to spend and be spent for the cause of Christ."[48]

In his work in Georgia and South Carolina Huckins made many friends and became their trusted colleague, even though he had been born and had always lived in the North. One such friend was the distinguished and influential Baptist minister Jesse Mercer. An ardent advocate of education, Mercer was born in North Carolina in 1769, but had lived in Georgia since he was six. He began preaching while still in his teens and had pastored churches for half a century.[49]

Through the years Mercer contributed his talents and energies to various Baptist educational endeavors in Georgia as well as in the District of Columbia. In recognition of his leadership, the Baptist manual labor school established in Georgia by the state convention in 1832 was named Mercer Institute, becoming Mercer University in 1838.[50]

Now the senior editor of the *Christian Index,* which he had purchased in 1833, Mercer encouraged the Baptists in that state to support the cause of the American Baptist Home Mission Society and its agent James Huckins. Huckins, he emphasized, was a "brother of good preaching talents, and associated with the South, in regard to the fanatical principles of northern Abolitionists."[51]

Huckins was extremely happy in his work and felt that "No field of usefulness [is] greater than the one I occupy. I have enjoyed Christ's presence and that is the only thing which keeps me up."[52]

During the first half of 1839, as Huckins visited various churches in Georgia and the Carolinas, the cause of Christ in Texas began to receive greater attention among the Baptist in the United States. Many denominations had preachers and missionaries in this infant republic, but Baptists lagged behind in establishing denominational work within its borders. Letters frequently appeared in Baptist publications encouraging the denomination's involvement there, especially since it was perceived by many that a large proportion of the residents in Texas were of the Baptist persuasion.

Baptist ministers, of course, had preached in Texas sporadically since the mid-1820s, only a short time after Stephen F. Austin had taken his colony to the then Spanish-ruled territory. Although all immigrants into Texas were supposed to become aligned with Catholicism, most did so nominally. Only a very few actually ever embraced that faith.

In 1836 when Texas won her independence from the Mexican government, the way was opened for the spread of Protestantism in the Lone Star Republic. Though Methodists and Presbyterians formed the majority of immigrant missionaries, there were a few Baptist ministers in Texas at that time. Perhaps the best known was the Reverend Z. N. Morrell, a rugged pioneer preacher from West Tennessee.

Born in 1803 in South Carolina, Morrell had preached in Tennessee for fourteen years when, in 1834, he was advised to move to a better climate for his health. He wanted to go to Texas to recuperate, but "the iron arm of Catholicism was stretched over the whole land of Mexico, then embracing the State of Texas, [and] did not make it a very desirable field for a Baptist preacher who had always been accustomed to express himself boldly and independently." He and his family, therefore, went to

Yellabusha County, Mississippi, to await an appropriate occasion to emigrate.[53]

In the early part of December 1835, Morrell joined a handful of friends for the 250-mile horseback trip to Texas. Arriving a few days before Christmas, he visited several locations and then journeyed back to Mississippi to superintend his family's move. His return to Texas in April 1836 coincided with the eastward flight of many of the residents who were fleeing from the threat of Mexican forces following the massacre at the Alamo.

Although occasions for preaching were scarce, even after the Mexican yoke had been thrown off, Morrell made the most of each opportunity, becoming the first person to preach in many Texas settlements.[54] One of these was in Washington-on-the-Brazos where he established a small church in 1837. In November of that year a committee of that church sent a letter to the American Baptist foreign mission society requesting consideration of Texas as a mission field. The letter implored the Baptist denomination to send ministers to Texas to serve as agents of the mission society in the towns of Washington, San Augustine, Nacogdoches, and San Antonio. The church promised financial assistance when possible.[55]

To ensure that their request was heard, the Washington church committee made several copies of their petition and mailed them to friends in the United States. One of these letters was sent to the Reverend S. G. Jenkins who lived in Mississippi and was a brother of committee member J. R. Jenkins. The Reverend Jenkins forwarded the request to the *Christian Index* in Georgia, which published it in February 1838.

The petition of the Washington church eventually reached the executive committee of the American Baptist Home Mission Society, who responded by requesting Morrell to accept a missionary commission. When he would not do so, they sought assistance from David Orr, a pioneer missionary in Arkansas. Orr made plans to go to Texas, but the move was never accomplished.[56]

Although interest in mission work in Texas remained high among Baptists in the States for the next several months, no official body made any formal commitment toward the work.

Without denominational support for the efforts in Texas, the difficulty of carving out an existence in this new frontier gradually took its toll. After a brief existence, the Washington church all but dissolved and the Baptist work in the republic virtually disappeared. Other denominations, however, sustained their operations in Texas through organized programs and financial assistance from their home bases in the United States.

IN MAY 1839 HUCKINS attended the eighteenth anniversary of the Georgia Baptist Convention.[57] At this meeting held in Richland, William M. Tryon was a messenger from the Alabama Baptist State Convention. A native of New York, Tryon had come to Georgia while in his late teens, both for his health and to engage in his trade of tailoring. In December 1832, at the age of twenty-three, he joined the First Baptist Church in Augusta, which subsequently licensed him to preach.[58] The next month he entered the first class of the newly created Mercer Institute at Penfield as one of approximately thirty students.[59] He studied there for three years before going to Texas in December 1835 for a brief visit.[60]

Returning early the next year, he was appointed an agent of the Georgia Baptist Convention,[61] in which capacity he served collecting money for mission and educational purposes, until the fall of 1837. At that time he assumed the pastorate of the newly organized Baptist church at Irwinton, Alabama.[62] The next year he added to his responsibilities the pastorate of the Bethlehem Baptist Church in Barbour County, Alabama.

Whether Tryon and Huckins met and discussed religious conditions in Texas is not known, but in his July report to the executive committee of the Home Mission Society, Huckins's increased interest in the Lone Star Republic became evident as he volunteered to leave his responsibilities in the South and go to Texas to ascertain that region's potential for mission work.[63] The society, eager to expand its work westward, favored his request. In the first week of November 1839 they voted to employ him for at least four months as a missionary to the young republic.[64] His assignment was to take a survey of the religious condition and to acquire such information of the state of public and private sentiment with regard to missions from our denomination, as may enable us in the future to prosecute operations in that country somewhat more nearly commensurate with our duty and its necessities.[65]

He was not to be confined to one particular location, but was to visit as much of the republic as feasible and then report back to the society.

As Huckins began making preparations in New York for his tour of Texas, he grew unhappy over the prospects of leaving his family once again and wrote his wife who was in Providence,

Pray for me dear wife, I feel melancholy and alone. Ah, it seems to be as tho I could not endure this trial of being separated from wife and children.... It throws the blood back to the heart and produces a sensation unutterable. God's will however be done. I hope that I may do good.[66]

On 17 November, Huckins began the long sea voyage to the Lone Star Republic. Even before any communication could reach Texas that a missionary agent was on the way, the stage was being set there for Huckins's ministry. On 28 November, David Wright, a businessman in Galveston, wrote his father who lived in New York to share his thoughts on the need for organized Baptist work in that city. In this letter the younger Wright stated that Galveston had two thousand people, but only "one clergyman, and he a Presbyterian, a good man; but he wants, to say the least, a good Baptist brother to assist him." Wright emphasized the immediacy of the situation as well as the willingness of many in the city to help defray the living expenses of a Baptist minister. "Our cry," he stated, "is send us a laborer, a willing laborer he must be, and look for his reward in heaven."[67]

A few days later Wright wrote his father again, stressing that the influx of immigrants—twelve hundred in the preceding week—made the need for a Baptist minister even more urgent. "Now is the time to get a foothold," he stressed, "and it should be done without delay. Send us a faithful minister of Jesus Christ."[68]

As Wright's letters were moving eastward for delivery, Huckins was slowly progressing westward, making stops along the way to share his plans with different Baptist groups. On 7 December he attended the Baptist State Convention in Beaufort, South Carolina, where he received a small contribution.[69] He then made several other stops before reaching New Orleans on 19 January 1840. In his personal travel journal he described New Orleans as having a population of one hundred thousand, with river traffic equal to New York.[70] He was impressed with the hotel facilities, sugar plantations, and orange groves, but expressed great concern about the lack of Baptist activities there. He wrote,

> the other denominations have already gained a strong foothold, and yet the Baptists have not a single church, not even a preacher. And why is it? The Presbyterians are ready to receive us with open arms—ready to aid us in sustaining a minister. We have a considerable number of communicants of a very respectable character, besides a very large number who are Baptists from education. These are ready to sacrifice liberally in order to sustain a holy and enlightened ministry.[71]

Huckins also indicated in his journal that he would pledge to raise one thousand dollars to sustain a minister, if the American Baptist Home Mission Society also would contribute five hundred dollars toward the project. He added, "In two years, with the blessing of God, the denomination in New Orleans would be amply able to sustain itself."[72]

While in New Orleans Huckins obtained a letter of introduction from H. H. Furman to Judge Benjamin C. Franklin in Galveston.[73] Franklin, a native of Georgia, had been active in Texas's struggle for independence from Mexico and had fought in the battle at San Jacinto. Following the establishment of the government of the republic, he had been appointed a district judge, serving in that capacity until November 1839, when he moved to Galveston to enter private law practice.[74]

HUCKINS LEFT NEW ORLEANS on 22 January aboard the *Neptune,* a 220-foot-long steamer "with 30 cabin passengers and 41 in steerage, bound for Texas, the land of promise and hope."[75] At about 6 P.M. on 24 January, Galveston "hove in view" and "joy lighted in every countenance."[76] From the sea the city could have easily been mistaken for a magnificent metropolis with elegant white marble residences, but what Huckins discovered in reality was a "poor straggly collection of weather-boarded frame houses, beautifully embellished with whitewash."[77]

The thirty-mile-long island that formed a part of the Texas coast had played a unique role through the years in the seafaring lives of various explorers, travelers, and privateers, providing them temporary shelters as well as hidden havens from the authorities. It was not, however, until the Texans' victory over the Mexicans at San Jacinto, which assured the region's independence, that the island attained substantial importance.

Michel F. Menard had obtained a land grant of about forty-six hundred acres of the island from the Mexican government. When Texas became a republic, he secured title to the same land from the Texas Congress. He then established the Galveston City Company to help develop the area.[78] Attempts to build a city had been countered by periodic violent storms that washed away most of the structures on the island, leaving it looking like a long sand bar with a handful of trees standing amidst scattered wreckage of ships and flimsy buildings. In addition to onslaughts by the weather, residents had been plagued by snakes, relentless invasions of blowing sand, and the devastating disease of yellow fever. Despite these almost constant adversities, the inhabitants continually rebounded and rebuilt in an effort to make Galveston the "pearl of Texas." By January 1839, when the city was chartered by the Texas government, its future as a most important port in the Lone Star Republic seemed assured. Only Velasco, Matagorda, and Houston offered even minor competition for the commerce that plied the seas to the young nation.[79]

In May of that year there were about three hundred houses accommodating the island's population of nearly two thousand. Several small public buildings existed, including a customhouse, courthouse, commissary and naval storehouse, market, magazine, arsenal, and hospital. There were also fifteen retail stores, six licensed taverns, two printing offices, several professional offices, and numerous shops for craftsmen and dry goods. Three hotels were being constructed to join the two already in operation, and two wharves and a pier neared completion.[80]

The fall of 1839 brought hundreds more immigrants to the Texas coast, many of whom stayed in Galveston. By January 1840, the population of the city was nearly three thousand, yet Galveston was still primitive in many ways. Its streets were but wide passages, usually ankle deep in sand, its lanes were covered with high grass, and intersecting open ditches served for drainage. There were no springs of fresh water, and most residents had to dig shallow wells to collect rain water.[81]

This was the Galveston that stood ready to greet James Huckins, the first Baptist missionary to arrive in Texas. Though not completely "civilized," the city was bristling with activity and its citizens were bounding with hope.

2

AS THE *NEPTUNE* DREW NEAR THE WHARF, which extended some sixty yards out from the shore, Huckins and others on board were impressed by the size of the crowd there on the "tiptoe of expectation, waiting the arrival of news, friends and strangers."[1] Most of the passengers disembarked as soon as the ship tied up, but Huckins, not expected by anyone or anticipating meeting any person he knew there, decided to rest on the ship that Friday evening and start for Houston the next day.[2]

In the morning, as Huckins left the ship dressed in his high white collar, black scarf tie, and dark coat with black velvet lapels, he unexpectedly met a friend whom he had baptized a couple of years earlier.[3] The two men breakfasted together. Then Huckins was introduced to several Baptists living in the city, including two who had been members of the First Baptist Church of Calais, Maine, when Huckins had been pastor there. After meeting with these friends, Huckins was requested to stay and preach the next day and "to collect the scattered sheep of Christ's flock."[4] He willingly complied and on Sunday morning preached to a group of more than two hundred at the Presbyterian church, which only recently had been organized. During his sermon Huckins noted an unusual solemnity within the congregation.

> The countenances of male and female indicated deep interest, mellowness of feeling, and with many, very many, the indications of a crushed spirit and fallen hopes were too clear to prevent deception. When home, or native land, or kindred afar off, or the uncertainty of earthly objects were referred to the tears would gush forth.[5]

That afternoon he preached to another large crowd and again in the evening when all "that could be seated were seated, and all that could stand, did stand, and many with heavy hearts were forced to retire for want of room."[6] Following the close of the evening service Huckins asked the Baptists and "all friendly to the denomination" to remain and meet with him. About twenty-five accepted his invitation. When he showed them his credentials and explained the object of his mission, the "united voice of all was 'Stay! O stay, and form us into a church!'"[7] Agreeing to this request, Huckins spent the next few days making preparations to organize the group into a church and visiting others who, he had been told, were friendly to the Baptist cause and might be potential prospects for membership.

On Thursday evening, 30 January 1840, he met with a group at the home of Thomas H. Borden to organize the first Baptist church in Galveston. After a hymn and a prayer, six people presented their church letters and became the nucleus of the new congregation. Three others who did not have their letters in hand also applied for membership and, after relating their Christian experience, were admitted.[8] These nine individuals, constituting the charter membership of the church, then elected Huckins, Francis W. Pettygrove, and George Fellows to draft Articles of Faith and the Church Covenant. Pettygrove had been a member of the First Baptist Church of Calais, Maine, and Fellows was from the First Baptist Church of Deerfield, New Hampshire.[9]

Immediately after the formal organization, Gail Borden, Jr., an agent of the Galveston City Company, and his wife, Penelope, daughter of Eli Mercer, who was a cousin of Huckins's friend Jesse Mercer, presented themselves as candidates for membership. The charter members voted to accept them on condition that they be baptized.

The next Sunday, Huckins preached at the courthouse, where the constitution of the Galveston Baptist Church was officially approved by the congregation. In recording this event in his journal Huckins wrote,

> When the little band came forward to receive the hand of fellowship, the effect was overwhelming. The spirit

of the church and congregation seemed literally to break down. Tears were profusely poured forth and the weeping in many cases became audible. It was a blessing so entirely unexpected, and yet one for which they had so long prayed, that their gratitude and joy were overwhelming.[10]

The following Tuesday afternoon Gail and Penelope Borden, along with her sister who had been accepted for membership since the organization of the church the previous week, gathered with the congregation and numerous onlookers on one of the southern beaches of the island. Their baptism would be the first to be conducted in the Gulf of Mexico west of the Mississippi River.

Borden, nearing forty years of age, was an enthusiastic and enterprising individual. Born in New York, he had lived in Indiana and Ohio as a youth. His frail health had led him south in hopes of a better climate. In 1822 he had settled in Mississippi, where he taught school briefly and then did survey work for the county and the United States government.

One of his students was sixteen-year-old Penelope Mercer, whom Borden later married.[11] In 1829 Borden and his wife joined her parents in a move to Texas, where Borden soon became active in politics and was appointed by Stephen F. Austin to superintend the official surveys of the colonies and to direct the Land Office at San Felipe. By August 1835, with the Mexican threat of invasion growing imminent, Borden, his brother Thomas, and Joseph Baker had developed plans to publish a newspaper. Two months later, the first issue rolled off the press under the name of *The Telegraph and Texas Register*.[12]

Following the Texans' victory over the Mexicans in April 1836 and the establishment of Sam Houston's administration, Borden was appointed first Collector of the Port of Galveston, making him responsible for the receipt of revenues and tariffs. In 1839 he was elected a city alderman and also an agent of the Galveston City Company.[13] He was to become one of the city's leading citizens and a significant influence in the Baptist movement in Texas.

Borden and Penelope had waited more than ten years for "some servant of Christ of their own faith to come and preach to them the word of life and baptize them." Huckins was the first they had met.[14] Even though they had not been involved in public worship services since being in Texas, they were accustomed to spending the Sabbath in reading and prayer.[15]

The baptismal service in the rolling waters off the sandy Galveston beach that afternoon proved to be a very emotional occasion. When it was over, the "congregation dispersed in too solemn a mood for conversation, disposed to commune with their own hearts."[16] Huckins's journal entry of that day indicated the significance that the ordinance had for him. He stated

> This day has been one of the happiest of my life. God has given me the privilege of baptizing three individuals. Never before since the creation of man have the waters of the great gulf this side of the Mississippi been visited for the performance of a rite so sacred. As long as life shall last I will cherish that scene, and it seems to me that my spirit in eternity will love to linger around its portraiture.[17]

Huckins remained in Galveston about two more weeks. During that time separate prayer meetings for the men and women of the church were initiated, a subscription for a building fund was started, and seven more people—five of them Negroes—were unified with the little congregation.

Realizing the imperativeness of his departure from the city to investigate the religious needs of other sections of the republic, Huckins wrote to Jesse Mercer to explain the emotional turmoil he was experiencing.

> Next week I must leave for the interior. But how can I do it? . . . O, could you hear the entreaties which come from our little church for me to stay with them, you would be prepared to conceive the feelings of the apostle when he said, 'Why will ye weep and break my heart?' but I must leave them, hoping and praying that

they may not long be destitute—that a man of God who will devote himself exclusively to preaching Christ may be sent to them. I know not of any field which promises greater improvement, or in which better materials for a church are to be found than in Galveston.[18]

Finally, after staying twenty-five days when he only had expected to pass through Galveston in a few hours, Huckins left for Houston, a forty-mile boat trip across Galveston Bay and up the narrow twisting Buffalo Bayou. Founded in 1836, Houston had served as the capital of the Republic of Texas from April 1837 to September 1839, when the government was moved to Austin. It had grown rapidly because of its preeminence as the capital city, and this growth had brought with it people from all walks of life, espousing divergent philosophies. Many of the citizens were virtuous, but many more were seemingly afflicted with multiple vices.

Although evangelistic preaching occasionally had been heard in the city since the Reverend Z. N. Morrell had spoken there in 1837, the influence of Christianity was not very conspicuous, and Huckins's first impression was disheartening.[19] He found a city of about three thousand people, few of whom were interested in the "purifying influences of religion."[20] The Presbyterians and Methodists had small congregations there, but these handfuls were not exerting much Christian influence.

As he surveyed the situation, Huckins concluded that the greatest obstacles to the cause of Christ in Houston were the false ministers and charlatans who were leading the people astray and some of the Christians who were living lives of sin.[21] In a letter to the Mercer University Mission Society he indicated, "No denomination can boast here, for they are all dishonored, and are all mourning."[22]

During the next few days he located several Baptists living in the city, and on Sunday morning, 23 February 1840, he conducted a worship service with them. That evening he interviewed all the individuals privately and encouraged each to unite in a group for weekly prayer meetings. Though sensing a great need in Houston and wishing to remain longer, Huckins felt he should continue his inspection of the religious conditions throughout the republic. Since his arrival in Texas, he frequently had heard accounts of people living in settlements on the Brazos and Colorado rivers. Some of the settlers had been praying for several months just to hear a Baptist minister preach, while others had been waiting for many years to be baptized. Moved by such reports, Huckins left Houston at the end of the month and traveled inland by horseback to visit these communities.[23]

His introduction to the Texas interior was a pleasant one, and as he rode he was "enraptured by the surrounding works of God."[24] To him the sky seemed to embrace the boundless prairie that was just beginning to come to new life. Watching the herds of wild horses and cattle and the huge flocks of ducks and geese made his journey the more enjoyable. The deer and their fawns, sporting in the fresh-growing grass, reminded him of the little lambs on the green hills of Vermont that he had witnessed as a youth. The total scene, "so crowded with animal and vegetable life," was something that he had never before encountered.[25]

After about eighteen miles he stopped at a small log cabin not far from a settlement to ask directions. There he met a man and his wife who informed him of about twenty families living in the next settlement who longed to hear a Baptist minister. The couple entreated him to stay and preach to all of them. As the next day was Sunday, he agreed, provided that they would be responsible to locate a suitable place to hold the service.

It was late as Huckins continued his journey. He had to cross streams and swamps in almost total darkness before he reached the home of an old friend who had not seen a preacher or heard a sermon since coming to Texas many years earlier. When Huckins finally arrived, her joy at seeing him "was more than sufficient to compensate for all the dangers and hardships" of his trip.[26]

The next day he fulfilled his commitment to the couple who had given him directions the preceding afternoon and preached to the large crowd they had assembled in the small settlement. He was amazed that the man and his wife had been able to get word of the preaching service to so many in the community, not realizing that the people's hunger to hear a Christian message had kept many up late the evening before riding to neighbors' homes to pass the word.

For the next several weeks Huckins journeyed to other towns and settlements along the Brazos and Colorado rivers, often riding all day in the rain and even sleeping on the lonely prairie when necessary. During his travels he was constantly inspired by the handiwork of God in nature and felt a remarkable calm. Since childhood he had had an unusual fear of wild animals, but as he rode through the forests where many ferocious animals roamed he was not afraid. He remained calm and resolute, allowing nothing to deter him from his mission.[27]

In the course of his travels, Huckins frequently had opportunities to preach and to baptize many who had been waiting for several years for a Christian minister to come their way.

AT LA GRANGE, ONE OF THE SMALL TOWNS on the Colorado River, Huckins met Robert Emmett Bledsoe Baylor, a native Kentuckian who had been living in Texas for about a year. Baylor's father and uncle both had had distinguished careers in the Revolutionary War, and he himself had served with two of his brothers in the War of 1812.

Baylor had studied law in Kentucky under his uncle, Jesse Bledsoe, and in 1819 had been elected to that state's legislature. The following year he moved to Tuscaloosa, Alabama, to practice law. Four years later he was chosen to serve in the Alabama legislature, and from 1829 to 1831 he represented the middle district of the state in the Twenty-first United States Congress. After his service as a member of the U.S. House of Representatives, Baylor returned to Alabama to continue his practice of law.

During the summer of 1839, Baylor, then forty-six years old, was converted at a revival service of the Talladega County Baptist Church, and shortly thereafter was licensed to preach. Within a few months he emigrated to Texas, hoping to spread the Gospel, to practice law, and to claim the land to which his late nephew, John Walker Baylor, was entitled because of his military service during the Texas revolution. The younger Baylor had been wounded at the Battle of San Jacinto and had later died in Alabama while on medical furlough.[28]

When Huckins first met Baylor, he was living in a "rude log hut" and operating a school to educate the children of the settlers who were crowding into La Grange, having been driven from their homes on the frontier by the continual threat of hostile Indians and Mexicans. Baylor's "rugged" clothes so distressed Huckins that he immediately made arrangements for a new suit of clothes to be made for Baylor by a merchant in Houston.[29]

Another minister in the La Grange area with whom Huckins became acquainted was the Reverend Thomas W. Cox, pastor of the Baptist church in Talledega from December 1836 until the summer of 1838.[30] Cox had been in Texas slightly more than a year and had recently organized a church at Travis, which he was pastoring along with the Independence church that had been established in the fall of 1839.

Huckins was only in La Grange a short time when he and Cox formed a presbytery on 25 March 1840, to constitute a Baptist church there.[31] His participation in its establishment must have greatly impressed the thirteen-member congregation for soon after the church was organized, they requested R. E. B. Baylor, who was probably attending church there, to write the American Baptist Home Mission Society to express their gratitude for Huckins. In his letter Baylor thanked the society for Huckins and urged the executive committee to "Send us clergymen of the right stamp, men of high moral bearing, and above all, men of vital piety; none others can do much good here." He also informed the society of several less-than-dedicated ministers then working in Texas, indicating that because of their activities "our blessed religion has been wounded and the only way to wipe off the stains is to give us pastors, like Caesar's wife, not only pure, but above suspicion."[32]

That spring Huckins completed his investigative tour, having visited most of the populated districts of the republic. In the report of his findings to the Home Mission Society, he indicated that he believed the potential for Baptist mission work in the republic was extremely favorable and stated that, "If we had the services of a few good missionaries in whom the public could confide, we might have twenty-two Baptist churches in Texas, as soon as the work of collecting an organization could be entered upon."[33]

HUCKINS'S REPORT AND HIS IMPASSIONED pleas regarding the needs of the people in Texas provided the impetus for the Home Mission Society's decision to establish a permanent base in the republic.[34] In its published review of the various mission stations under its sponsorship, the society emphasized the dramatic needs in Texas and the various appeals for assistance that had been received from residents of the republic. The executive committee urged that these calls for help be answered by those who felt so impressed. They stated that "the Society is ready to send suitable men; and the denomination would nobly sanction the act: but they know of none to send; none signify a readiness to go."[35]

Though the Mission Society knew of no one who was considering becoming a missionary to the Republic of Texas, there was an individual who for some time had been contemplating going there to preach the Gospel. He was William Tryon, currently pastor of the Baptist church in Wetumpka, Alabama. He had served this church since leaving Irwinton in January 1840, and though he considered his ministry in Wetumpka highly important, the needs of Texas lay heavy on his heart. During the summer or early fall he contacted the Mission Society in New York to obtain information regarding appointment as a missionary to the Lone Star Republic.[36]

Huckins's original commission from the Home Mission Society had been for a four-month investigative tour of Texas to ascertain the potential for Baptist work there. Because of the needs and prospects evidenced in his reports, the society had requested Huckins to travel extensively throughout the south and east to raise funds for future Texas work.

Upon his return to the states in May 1840 Huckins faithfully undertook this task, staying so busy during the summer that he did not have an opportunity even to visit his wife who had remained in Providence during his tour of Texas. In fact, his first occasion to be with her did not occur until 5 September, when, after a ten-month separation, they accidentally met at the train station in New York City. Unfortunately, their reunion lasted only twenty-four hours as Huckins had an engagement in Poughkeepsie the next day, and Rhoda had to return to her parents' home in Providence.[37]

Huckins was a very effective speaker, and his discourses on the religious needs in Texas usually impressed his audiences. As he continued through the early fall to share information about the spiritual wantonness in the young republic, he became so burdened for the people there himself that he felt called to return. Thus in October 1840, he applied to the Home Mission Society for reappointment as a missionary to Texas. The society favorably responded and renewed his commission the next month, agreeing to pay him about four hundred dollars for a year's labor and also to provide the necessary funds to transport his family and furnishings to Texas.[38]

Because of the primitive conditions that he knew faced his family in Galveston, Huckins offered his wife the privilege of remaining in Providence for another year. She declined, however, because she was convinced that their family needed to be together and become settled in Texas as soon as possible. She also felt that the Galveston congregation would feel more comfortable with Huckins as their pastor if his family were with him.[39]

Shortly after his recommissioning, a special prayer meeting was held for Huckins and his family at the Oliver Street Baptist Church in New York City. Established in the 1790s, the church was well known for its support of mission endeavors. Since 1825, when Spencer Cone had become pastor, the church had been a rallying center for the friends of foreign missions, holding concerts of prayer every month.[40]

At the prayer service, the Oliver Street congregation was joined by members from other churches in the city. Following addresses by local pastors, Huckins spoke "in a feeling manner upon the trials and difficulties peculiar to his field of labor, and showed the important points to which he desired the prayers" to be directed.[41] His reception by the people at the meeting seemed to assure him of their continual support during his impending sojourn in Texas.

3

HUCKINS, HIS WIFE, and their young daughters, Caroline and Sarah, sailed for the Lone Star Republic the second week of December 1840. While they were en route, William Tryon—who earlier that month had been appointed a missionary by the Home Mission Society—was raising money in Alabama to help finance his own trip to Texas which was scheduled for January.[1]

During the two-week journey to Galveston, Huckins became extremely ill. The family had brought with them materials for a one-and-a-half-story house, but due to Huckins's illness was unable to start construction. They, therefore, moved in with Gail and Penelope Borden in their small cottage near the beach.

When William Tryon and his wife arrived in Galveston three weeks later on 18 January 1841, Huckins was still suffering from his malady. His usual buoyancy and enthusiasm had dissipated, and his frail and weak condition worried Tryon. Because of his incapacitation, Huckins thus far had been unable to select an appropriate city in which Tryon could begin his labors. Tryon's assistance had been requested by Baptists of both Matagorda and Independence, but Huckins had not yet investigated either place to determine which had the greater need. He, therefore, sent Tryon to Houston to get acclimated to life in the frontier republic, with instructions to wait there until he could confer with him about any future assignment.[2]

Around the first of February, even though he had not completely recovered, Huckins went to Houston to meet with Tryon, and after some deliberation it was decided that Tryon should begin his work at Independence. Huckins then returned to Galveston where he and his family moved into a small house on the east end of the island while making preparations for the construction of their own home. In March Huckins assumed the pastorate of the Baptist church in Galveston,[3] and the next month constituted a group of Baptists in Houston into a church.[4] This congregation shortly afterward also called him to be their pastor.[5] For the next several months he preached to both the Houston and Galveston churches as well as to Baptists in various towns along the Brazos and Trinity rivers.

During this same period William Tryon's influence began to be felt in several areas of the republic, one of which was in Washington-on-the-Brazos where he reestablished the Baptist Church that had collapsed in 1838 shortly after sending requests to the mission societies in the United States for ministerial assistance in Texas. He also preached in Matagorda—the first Baptist minister to do so—conducted a sweeping revival at Mt. Gilead Baptist Church in Washington County, constituted the Providence church in Milam County, and became the full-time pastor of the Independence church that he had co-pastored for a while with the Reverend Thomas W. Cox. Because Cox lived in La Grange, about sixty miles from Independence, the two men had agreed that Tryon could better serve the Independence congregation, since he had settled near that town.[6]

With the success being enjoyed by Huckins and Tryon, as well as by R. E. B. Baylor and other Baptist ministers in Southeast Texas, the outlook of the denomination's influence seemed most promising, and a spirit of harmony prevailed in the activities of the churches. However, this unison was short-lived when a rift developed over doctrinal matters during the second annual meeting of the Union Baptist Association in October 1841.

It was not the first discord associated with this body, for in June 1840, during the initial attempt to form the first cooperative Baptist organization in Texas, controversies between missionary and anti-missionary interests disrupted the proceedings to such an extent that no agreement on organization could be reached. The following October the missionary-minded group met separately and formed an association. At this meeting only the churches of Travis, Independence, and La Grange—each pastored by Cox and having a total membership of only forty-five—were represented. The Reverend Z. N. Morrell, pastor of the Plum

Grove church, largest Baptist congregation in the republic, had planned to attend, but was unable to do so because of illness. Though there were several other churches then in existence in Texas, they did not send representatives to the gathering.[7]

The ten delegates present chose Cox as moderator, J. W. Collins, clerk, and R. E. B. Baylor, corresponding secretary. The Articles of Faith they adopted emphasized the missionary approach to the spread of the Gospel as opposed to the predestinarian, anti-missionary philosophy.[8] Cox, though a believer in the missionary practice, was also a proponent of Campbellism, a faith that required baptism as essential to salvation. His embracement of this belief was not widely known at that time, but soon after the formation of the association, he began publicly affirming his Campbellite views.

When the second annual session of the Union Association met at the Clear Creek Meeting House near Rutersville on 8 October 1841, Cox, pastor of the host church, preached the opening sermon and issued an invitation for those interested to join the church. Huckins and Tryon publicly objected because they felt his views to be strongly pro-Campbellite. After an open debate the reception of potential members was postponed.[9] Although the controversy over Cox's views was heated, it did not seem to dampen the enthusiasm and spirit of the associational meeting since the delegates continued their deliberations and formed several committees to promote the Baptist faith.

Several ministers were called upon to address the delegates. Among them was James Huckins, who took the opportunity to discuss the organization and operations of the American Baptist Home Mission Society. In addition, he requested a committee of six to aid him in "determining the most suitable points for stationing the missionaries, who may hereafter be sent amongst us by the said society."[10]

Although it was Huckins's first time to participate in a meeting of this nature in Texas, his leadership was recognized by his colleagues. When the association created the Texas Home Mission Society, he was named its president. He also was chosen to serve as the head of an agency to supply the denomination with books, and was named a member of the executive committee. He was also requested to preach the introductory sermon at the next annual meeting of the association and to write the circular letter that would be distributed to churches throughout the republic and in many areas of the United States.[11]

The association also named Huckins to the Education Committee, along with W. H. Ewing and a Mr. Green. Later in the sessions the delegates approved this committee's recommendation that an education society be formed to "assist in procuring an education for those young men who give evidence of being called of God to preach the Gospel, and who shall have the approbation of their respective churches."[12] Several large tracts of land were pledged to support the establishment of "an academical and theological institution" under the administration of this society.[13]

In the fall of 1840, the editor of the *Baptist Banner and Western Pioneer,* a weekly newspaper published in Louisville, Kentucky, and widely distributed throughout the southern United States, had suggested that someone from the then newly formed Union Association become the editor of a Texas column for this publication. Although the newspaper editor had suggested R. E. B. Baylor for the position, the Union Association had never made a definite decision regarding it. At this second session of the association the proposal was once again considered and the representatives from the churches, trusting Huckins's ability, requested that he take over this unique responsibility.[14]

Following the conclusion of the association meeting, most of the participants returned to their places of service, but Morrell, who had been requested by Huckins and several others to present charges of heresy against Cox to the La Grange congregation at their next business meeting, remained. A few days later he presented his accusations, and, after heated debate, the church excluded Cox as their pastor.[15]

During the last few weeks of the year Huckins participated in numerous church and denominational affairs, including the ordination of A. A. Buffington, the second person to be ordained as a Baptist minister in Texas. Of all the leadership opportunities available in the denomination in 1841, Huckins had been called upon more than anyone else to assume them. It was evident that his ability was being recognized by his Baptist colleagues.

4

DURING THE FIRST TWO MONTHS OF 1842 Huckins preached regularly to the Galveston and Houston congregations and made frequent speeches before temperance societies, Masonic bodies, and interdenominational conferences. In March an intrusion into Texas by Mexican military forces dramatically affected his ministry.

The Mexicans who engaged in this attack were not trying to recapture Texas, whose loss their government had never formally acknowledged. Instead they were displaying a show of force in retaliation for the actions of a particular group of Texans the previous fall.

In the summer of 1841, Texas President Mirabeau B. Lamar, without congressional consent, had authorized a 321-man "army" to go to Santa Fe, New Mexico, to encourage the citizens of that city, thought to be languishing under Mexican misrule, to annex themselves to Texas for mutual political and commercial benefits. Unfortunately, these "Santa Fe Pioneers," as they were sometimes dubbed, suffered from faulty reconnaissance, insufficient provisions, and Indian harassment during their three-month journey. They eventually were ambushed and taken captive to Mexico City, where they experienced numerous indignities while incarcerated.[1]

In retaliation for the "impudence" of the infant republic, General Santa Anna, in early 1842, had directed General Rafael Vasquez to lead several hundred soldiers into Texas to plunder selected cities. The Mexican force crossed the border in March and easily captured San Antonio, Refugio, and Goliad from the unsuspecting and unprepared Texans.[2]

The invasion raised in many of the residents fears reminiscent of those that caused a mass evacuation before the forces of Santa Anna in 1836. This time, however, the Texans were determined to protect their homeland, and volunteers from throughout the country gathered arms and set out for San Antonio.

The women of Galveston abandoned their regular household chores and engaged in "moulding bullets and assisting in the military preparations."[3] Most of the men in the Baptist church in Houston banded together to ride to San Antonio and Victoria to fight the Mexicans. Every "man capable of bearing arms" was ordered "to be in readiness at a moment's warning."[4] Huckins was entreated by members of the Houston congregation to go with them. Although he realized the value of having a chaplain among the volunteers, he felt more obligated to his family and to the remaining members of his churches, and so he declined.[5]

Since the Mexican invasion was primarily an attempt to remind the Texans of the power of their southern neighbors, Vasquez withdrew his forces from San Antonio after only a few days and returned to Mexico. However, poor communication delayed this information and rumors ran rampant across Texas and into some parts of the United States. As a result, for weeks after Vasquez had crossed back over the Rio Grande River, volunteer groups in the republic and from the neighboring states continued to move toward the frontier to help drive the intruders from Texas soil. After learning that the Mexicans had, indeed, retreated, most Texas militiamen returned to their homes. But many of the volunteers from the United States lingered just to be on hand in the event of another Mexican sneak attack, some even hoping for an officially sanctioned invasion of Mexico.

By the middle of spring, as life gradually returned to a more normal pace, Huckins began preaching again in Galveston and Houston. Soon he expanded his ministry into the Fort Bend area. Fort Bend had been a frontier outpost during the early days of the republic and was located at a deep bend in the Brazos River, approximately twenty miles west of Houston. In 1837, when the territory was organized into a county, the name Fort Bend was selected and the following year the town of Richmond absorbed the Fort Bend settlement and became the county seat. Huckins had preached there while on his investigative tour in 1840, but had been disappointed by the response of the settlers.[6] Now, however, the response was more encouraging. He therefore decided to add the Richmond area to his regular circuit of responsibilities.

In a letter to the Home Mission Society, Huckins reported that he was going to "lay every other exciting topic aside" in an endeavor to make his ministry in Galveston, Houston, and Richmond more effective. He indicated that his prayer would be: "God grant that I may succeed."[7] He also informed the society that he was experiencing a great "increase of religious feeling" among the black congregations, which included about one hundred and fifty in both Galveston and Houston and about two hundred in Fort Bend.[8]

In May Huckins conducted a series of meetings in Montgomery County, one of the most populous and richest in the republic. While preaching to crowds of up to six hundred people, many who rode twenty-five to thirty miles to hear him, Huckins encountered several persons who felt "Montgomery County should be selected as the seat of our literary institution," the idea for which had arisen at the previous meeting of the Union Association. One planter even offered his plantation, worth at least thirty-five hundred dollars, as the site for the school.[9] However, since the association had not yet made an official commitment for an institution of this type, the offer was necessarily declined.

That summer, as Huckins traveled through the counties along the Colorado and Brazos rivers, the atmosphere of the republic was seemingly harmonious and peaceful. However, a mood of unrest was seething as the volunteers who had come to Texas in the spring and a considerable number of the local citizens clamored for an invasion of Mexico. Even those who did not wish to attack across the Rio Grande still remained on alert against possible Mexican threats.

The wisdom of this preparation was proven in September when General Santa Anna sent General Adrian Woll and approximately a thousand men back to Texas. This time the citizens of San Antonio had prepared themselves, but on 11 September, as General Woll approached, they recognized their inadequacy against the well-trained Mexican forces, and most of them evacuated the city.

As news of the recapture of San Antonio reached towns and settlements throughout the republic, once again bands of militia rushed to the scene to drive out the invaders. The citizens of Washington did not learn of the fate of San Antonio until Saturday, 17 September, but within "half an hour every man and boy of 15 or over who was able to go was hard at work cleaning his gun." By Monday morning very few men remained in the town and "even the Rev. W. M. Tryon headed for the frontier."[10]

The opposing forces met at Salado Creek, about six miles from San Antonio. The battle, although not a clear victory for either side, resulted in numerous Mexican casualties and caused the eventual retreat of General Woll. A short time later, a contingent of men invaded Mexico in an attempt to catch General Woll and free his prisoners, but this effort was most unsuccessful. It resulted only in the imprisonment and tragic deaths of many of the volunteers.

While many Texans were involved in the Mexican conflict, most of the citizens of Galveston were struggling to dig out from a devastating storm that had swept the city on 18 September. Numerous structures had been destroyed, including the Episcopal and the Methodist churches.[11]

The latter part of October was the time scheduled for the next annual gathering of the Union Baptist Association, but because of the country's unsettled condition, the meeting was postponed until the last week of November. Of the twelve churches that sent delegates to the session, two were pastored by Huckins and four by Tryon. In addition, Tryon co-pastored another with R. E. B. Baylor, who also preached at two others. Of the remaining churches, Morrell served two and the Reverend Noah Byars was the pastor of one. These congregations varied in size from ten to more than a hundred. The total membership of the association was four hundred thirty-three, a gain of approximately three hundred in the two years since its organization.

At the conference Huckins was picked for the special committee to revise the Articles of Faith, Constitution, and Rules of Decorum and was renamed to both the Book Committee and the Executive Committee. In addition, he was requested to preach the associational sermon the following year.[12]

EVEN THOUGH RELIGIOUS CONDITIONS were vastly improving in Texas in the early weeks of 1843, there was still a great spiritual void. Huckins attempted to fill this by expanding his ministry throughout much of the interior. In one of the oldest settlements in Brazoria County he became the first person ever to deliver a sermon.

He always was welcomed at plantations, especially by the slaves, with whom he seemed to have a unique rapport. His sermons on Sunday evenings were normally adapted "to the capacity of the Negroes," and after these services he usually gave them an opportunity to hold a prayer meeting in which he always participated. These meetings were "considered a kind of jubilee" by the slaves.[13]

In a report to the Home Mission Society of his activities during the first part of the year, Huckins was especially pleased with the results of his work at Fort Bend. He wrote,

> Here the morals of the people have undergone an entire change. Drunkenness, gambling, and horseracing have almost entirely disappeared, and an interest is being awakened upon the subject of religion.[14]

However, in spite of the receptiveness to the Gospel there, Huckins felt that Texas generally was a difficult place in which to minister. He informed the society's Executive Committee,

> You can form no conception of the destitution which prevails in many minds of anything like religious ideas. I have heard ignorance before upon the subject of religion, but I have never conceived of it, to the extent I have found it, in our frontier families. Even the most common expressions used in a sermon are not understood.[15]

To adapt his sermons to those with little knowledge of the scriptures or religious terminology was probably difficult for Huckins. He usually preferred a scholarly approach in writing his sermons and nearly always read from the pulpit. Huckins was considered by Morrell as a close thinker, who "from the pulpit presented his thoughts in the clearest manner, always exhibiting the fact that he was a profound scholar and student."[16] Another contemporary once described him as "the strongest man of the denomination and perhaps the most profound scholar."[17]

In spite of his sometimes staid approach and mechanical gestures, Huckins usually was well accepted and respected.

> He attracted great attention. And such was the force of his thought and the subject presented that one would almost forget everything else; his sermons abounded in gospel truth, were plain, pointed and practical, and generally showed mature previous preparation.[18]

Because of his successes in Brazoria and Fort Bend counties, Huckins devoted an almost disproportionate amount of time preaching in the interior compared with the time he spent in Galveston and Houston. The response of the frontier people and their hunger for the Gospel might have accounted for the greater amount of time he allotted them. In these outlying settlements he had opportunities to address very large audiences, while in the port cities his congregation were extremely small. Fortunately, the Galveston church members were not jealous of the time Huckins spent away from them, but rejoiced "that our pastor so far has succeeded in gaining the affection of the people not only in these counties, but of our brethren and friends generally throughout the country."[19]

Their willingness to share Huckins may have been somewhat influenced by their embarrassment that they had been unable to pay his salary for the past several months. In a letter to the Home Mission Society in March 1853, Gail Borden, who had recently been elected a vice president of the society, attributed this inability to the cost of "carrying on with war" against the Mexicans. The city had been required to pay more than twenty thousand dollars plus all the regular taxes to support the government's efforts to keep the republic free from a Mexican takeover. Borden, though disappointed that funds had been unavailable for Huckins's salary, nevertheless expressed hope that the congregation could raise enough in the future to pay at least a portion of it. He requested that the society recommission Huckins at a salary of six hundred dollars per year and assign him just to Galveston. If the society would honor this request, Borden stated, then the thirty-one-member church there would allow Huckins to "visit such distant sections of our country as might appear to him would best serve the great interest of Zion, and be most useful in establishing or building up churches."[20]

Although Huckins's current salary from the society was five hundred dollars per year, the inability of the Galveston congregation to provide assistance probably strained him financially. Therefore, in order to obtain additional income, he and his wife opened a school for young ladies and gentlemen in Galveston in April.[21]

Other institutions had previously operated in the city, the first a girls' school in 1838. It was soon replaced, and in 1840 James P. Nash had opened a school for boys emphasizing the "Three Rs" system of education.[22] None of these had been well accepted by the citizens of Galveston and as a result none had been very successful. Huckins's institution, however, known as the Galveston Academy, rapidly gained acceptance, and the revenue generated by its operation gradually helped to improve his financial condition. While superintending the school Huckins continued to preach in Galveston, Houston, and Richmond, as well as at various locations along the Brazos River.

DURING THE SPRING OF 1843, because of the growing publicity over the slavery issue, Huckins began to consider terminating his employment as a missionary of the American Baptist Home Mission Society. Since he had been in Texas the slavery controversy had continued to smolder throughout the United States, with occasional flare-ups in various religious and civic groups. Because the primary focus of the early immigrants to Texas had been the carving out of the wilderness a bare subsistence for themselves, the issue had not been of major concern to the majority of the citizens of the republic. Even though occasional abolitionists attracted attention in some of the cities—especially Houston and Galveston—they were usually soon forgotten, and life was little affected by their actions. However, there had been Baptist antislavery groups in the United States for some time, and, although their activities had influenced few major policies of the denomination, by the early 1840s their growing strength was becoming more noticeable.

In April 1840, at the first meeting of the American Baptist Anti-Slavery Convention, the delegates agreed to make a more concerted effort to diminish the influence of slavery in the nation.[23] In November of the same year, the Board of Managers of the Baptist General Convention expressed concern over the threat of some churches to withdraw financial support from the denomination's missionary programs because of differences over the slavery question. By the middle of 1841, both opponents and proponents of slavery seemed set for battle to protect and project their own interests.[24]

However, through skillful sidestepping and compromises, no major rifts had developed. Even so, the issue refused to die, and the antislavery sentiment continued to grow, especially in the North. It gradually became a religious issue as sermons and addresses in both the North and South frequently cited biblical authority as the basis of justification for both sides of the question.

The conflict over slavery soon encroached upon the heart of the missionary work in North America, and gradually Huckins was drawn into the midst of it. When he had been appointed an agent of the Home Mission Society in November 1838, his feelings regarding slavery were not a major concern, although they had played a decisive role in his leaving the church in Calais. After settling in Texas, Huckins felt a need to provide assistance for his wife and family because of the frequent absences from home which his travel schedule demanded. Therefore, he purchased a slave to assist with household chores.[25]

In late 1843 public inquiries and condemnations were made in northern newspapers regarding the holding of slaves by both Huckins and William Tryon. In 1840 Tryon had married a widow in Alabama who owned several slaves. After the couple had permanently settled in Texas, they used the slaves to work on their farm at Hidalgo Bluff near Washington-on-the-Brazos.

As the situation continued to worsen, with frequent bitter

editorials in the newspapers, Huckins felt that if he were no longer an appointee of the Home Mission Society, the controversy might subside. Therefore, in late spring 1843, with renewed faith both in the ability of the Galveston congregation to provide better financial support and the anticipated success of his academy, he resigned as a paid employee of the society, remaining on the roster as an unsalaried missionary. Tryon, however, remained under active appointment.[26]

Although Huckins was a slaveholder, this fact did not seem to hinder his acceptance by the black population. Huge crowds often flocked to hear him preach on the plantations and settlements in the interior, as well as in the city of Galveston. In fact, the Galveston church was 60 percent black.

The reason for Huckins's popularity among the Negroes may have been due in part to his physical characteristics. Slaves, situated at the bottom of the social strata, more easily identified with a person who had what some might consider physical flaws or unbecoming personal habits. Huckins's sallow complexion, prominent nose, crossed eye, and casual hair style, and his incessant use of tobacco, were imperfections that seemed to draw the underprivileged to him.

Another reason for his immense following among the Negroes may have related to the respect generated by his dedication to his work, especially among those who lived along the Brazos River. The slaves on these plantations deeply appreciated Huckins's willingness to give up time with his family and travel the lonely and dangerous miles to preach to them. They knew that often his health was poor and that he had had to leave his sick bed to visit them.

Combined with these "advantages" was the manner of his preaching. Even though he preferred doctrinally oriented sermons, to the Negroes he tried to preach with emotion in an effort to draw them closer to God. He felt it was "far better to let a congregation go away bowed down like a bulrush feeling that they were sinners than to be pleased with the preacher, the sermon or themselves."[27] The blacks, who were generally somewhat more emotionally inclined than their white masters, seemed to respond to this type of preaching.

Not only did Negroes favorably respond to Huckins's ministry, but the white members of his congregations also greatly admired and respected him. His ministerial colleagues often called upon him to preach for them and to lead protracted meetings.

Huckins was a tactful individual, conservative in his religious opinions, and displayed unusual skill in counseling people. He possessed great "personal magnetism, dauntless courage and was very resolute in purpose."[28] In addition he had untiring zeal, excellent powers of concentration, and an unusual ability to judge character.[29] These characteristics greatly aided him in his pastoral work where he obtained his greatest successes in one-to-one ministering.

Following his resignation from the Home Mission Society, Huckins continued to serve his Galveston, Houston, and Richmond congregations and to direct the operation of his academy.

5

AT THE FOURTH ANNUAL MEETING of the Union Association, held in October 1843, at the Providence Baptist Church in Washington County, Huckins was supposed to preach the associational sermon. He was unable to participate in the meeting, however, probably because of illness. It was the third time that Huckins had been scheduled to deliver either the associational or introductory sermon, and the third time that he had not done so.

In the 1841 and 1842 associational gatherings, last-minute changes in his schedule necessitated the substitution of other ministers to preach, an occurrence that was not unusual among Texas preachers. Often one scheduled to speak before religious audiences would request another minister to fulfill his responsibility, even if he were present. There was little jealousy among the ministers, and all seemed to enjoy hearing their colleagues preach, especially at protracted meetings where several usually had a chance to expound on the Gospel.

On one occasion Huckins was requested to substitute for a speaker who had failed to arrive. Though he protested that he could not preach because he had not brought any of his manuscripts from which to read, after earnest pleading by the crowd, he relented and "for the space of an hour he held the audience spellbound, by the force of his clear, burning thoughts."[1] Following his address, several people went to him to "give him permission to preach as often as he wished, even if his notes should be forgotten."[2]

Even though Huckins did not attend the 1843 meeting of the association, he did have a small part in the proceedings. At the previous conference he had been named to a special committee to study the Constitution, Articles of Faith, and Bill of Inalienable

Rights. This committee had met during the year. Its recommendations were presented to the delegates gathered at Providence church, and all were approved.

The significant changes that the committee suggested in the Articles of Faith involved the addition of a phrase in the article relating to baptism and the deletion of two articles that pertained to financial obligations of church members. The original article on baptism had dictated only that it be by immersion. The change added the phrase "performed by a regularly ordained Baptist minister in good standing."[3] The deleted articles had specified that it was the duty of the church to contribute to the pastor "of their worldly substance for his support and that of his family" and that the "pecuniary burdens of the church should be borne equally by all, according to the ability that God has given."[4]

The only major change in the Constitution was the incorporation of an article from the Bill of Inalienable Rights. This item guaranteed the autonomy of each individual church, a doctrine that was considered so fundamental that it was placed in the Constitution. With the addition of this article to the Constitution, the Bill of Inalienable Rights, containing only one other article, was abolished.

Shortly after the associational meeting, the Galveston and Houston congregations discontinued their regular worship services because of lingering disruptions and fears brought about by the Mexican invasions of the spring and fall of 1842. Apparently the people had become so concerned about their physical condition that they were able to give little thought to their spiritual welfare. Many even left the cities and moved to interior locations, which they felt were safer, and others made lengthy visits to friends in other parts of Texas or the United States.

Since the Houston and Galveston churches temporarily closed their doors, Huckins did not have many opportunities to preach to the Baptists in these cities for the next several months. He did continue to teach a large Bible class and occasionally spoke at services of other denominations.

It was during this time he began to recognize the value of a permanent church facility. The other denominations in Galveston had church buildings, funds for which had come from contributors in the United States, but the Baptists, prior to the suspension of their services, had usually met in Huckins's home, his academy, or in a rented room. Huckins realized that if he were going to be able to revive his dwindling church, a permanent worship structure would have to be among his first priorities.

On 2 December 1844, while Huckins was still considering ways by which a church building could be erected, the Ninth Congress of the republic of Texas convened at Washington-on-the-Brazos. One of the actions of that body would become the catalyst for the eventual addition of a new dimension to his life. This new "calling" as it would later be considered, would eventually promulgate Huckins into the forefront of educational fundraising among Texas Baptists.

THREE DAYS AFTER CHRISTMAS, a petition to charter a Baptist university was presented on the Senate floor. This petition was the culmination of the efforts of the Texas Baptist Education Society, which had been founded in 1841 by the Union Baptist Association. Because of the disrupted state of affairs, the society had not met formally in 1842 and 1843.[5] The 1844 officers were R. E. B. Baylor, president, William Tryon, vice-president, and J. G. Thomas, corresponding secretary. The society also had a treasurer and a board of managers. Huckins had been one of the original members of this board, but was not named to the 1844 slate of officers.[6]

At the fall 1844 meeting of the Education Society, Tryon and Baylor proposed the establishment of a literary institution in the republic.[7] This was not a new idea within the Baptist denomination, for several schools were operating in the United States under the auspices of the Baptists. Indeed, both Huckins and Tryon had attended Baptist institutions of higher education. Neither was it a new thought among Texas Baptists, for Huckins had discussed similar possibilities with friends in Montgomery County in 1842.[8] However, it was the first time that a proposal to establish a university had been presented for official consideration before any Baptist body in Texas since the subject was first broached at the 1841 meeting of the Union Association.

Individual Baptists had been leaders in the educational

movement in Texas for many years, some of them long before it became a republic. Among the earliest settlers of the country were a few Baptist preachers, and some of them had established and operated schools for varying periods of time. Even Morrell and Baylor had supplemented their income by teaching school, and Huckins was still superintending the Galveston Academy. All of the educational endeavors, however, were limited to preparatory institutions.

The plan Tryon and Baylor presented at the 1844 meeting of the Education Society involved education at both the preparatory and collegiate level. It was favored by the members of the Education Society, who voted to "found a Baptist University in Texas, upon a plan so broad that the requirement of existing conditions would be fully met, and that would be susceptible of enlargement and development to meet the demand of all ages to come."[9]

Several universities had been established in the republic of Texas, but most had lasted only a few years. Some had never opened their doors to students even after being chartered. Perhaps the most successful institution of higher learning still operating in the republic was Rutersville College, owned by the Methodist Conference. Others in operation at this time included one in San Augustine and another in Galveston.

The initial step to accomplish the society's goal of creating a university was to seek a charter from the Texas Congress. Though the requirements for obtaining a charter were not extremely complicated, specific procedures did have to be followed in order to achieve the desired result. Among them was the drafting of a petition and a proposed charter, which had to be adopted by both Houses of Congress. The charter then had to be approved by the Speaker of the House, President of the Senate, and President of the Republic.

R. E. B. Baylor, a district judge since his election in 1841, had been a member of the legislatures of Kentucky and Alabama as well as a U.S. congressman. He was unquestionably the most knowledgeable member of the Education Society regarding legislative matters. Recognizing this, the members of the society appointed Baylor to join Tryon and Thomas as a committee to seek the charter.

Tryon was personally acquainted with many of the representatives and senators, since he had unofficially served as Senate chaplain during the Seventh Congress and had formally been elected to the position in the Eighth Congress. The government had moved to Washington-on-the-Brazos in 1842 following General Woll's invasion, and Tryon lived only a few miles from the town. The legislators with whom he was not personally acquainted undoubtedly knew of him and his work.

Thomas, a trained lawyer, had just been elected clerk of the Union Association in August of that year and was new to his position as corresponding secretary of the Education Society. A native of Tennessee, he had come to Texas in 1841 and was a charter member of the Dove church, which had been constituted in Caldwell in May 1843. Extremely active in the denomination, he was contemplating becoming a minister.[10] How much value he was in helping to secure the charter is not known, but surely his rapport with the lawyers serving in Congress would have been of some assistance.

Shortly after the society had chosen the three-member committee, Baylor visited Tryon at his farm at Hidalgo Bluff. There the necessary documents for presentation to Congress were developed as Baylor dictated the words and Tryon recorded them on paper. The only part not completed when the materials were taken to the legislature for approval was the name by which the institution would be called.[11]

When the petition was under consideration by the Senate, the names San Jacinto University and Milam University were successively recommended by the lawmakers. On the final reading, however, the name Baylor University was recommended and approved. R. E. B. Baylor had originally suggested the name of Tryon for the institution, but Tryon declined. He feared that, since he had been working so strongly to establish a university in Texas, some might feel he had been doing so for his own personal gain. Tryon then suggested that the university be named for Baylor, who also demurred on the grounds that he had done nothing worthy to be so honored. However, Kenneth Anderson, newly inaugurated vice president of the republic, joined in support of Tryon's suggestion. Thus Baylor's name was accepted by the legislators.[12] On February 1, just two days before the session closed, Texas President Anson Jones approved the charter by affixing his signature.

Authority to direct the operation of the institution was given to fifteen trustees, most of whom had been associated with Baptist work in Texas for some time. Because of Huckins's prominence and leadership in the denomination, he was selected as one of the original trustees.[13]

Whether all fifteen trustees had been notified of their selection prior to the approval of the charter is not known, but shortly after the close of the Ninth Congress, several Texas newspapers carried the notice of the establishment of Baylor University and a call for the named trustees to assemble at Independence on 7 April 1845. Several trustees complied with the published request, but there were not enough to form a quorum. The inaugural meeting had to be postponed until the following month. Huckins was one of those who did not appear for the first session, perhaps because of renewed involvement in his church activities.

On 9 March 1845, after a lapse of almost two years, the Galveston Baptist Church had met in conference to discuss its future as a congregation. On this occasion Huckins related the story of the church's founding and traced its ragged history during its five-year existence. He also discussed his previous work as a missionary of the American Baptist Home Mission Society, emphasizing the important financial role that the society had played in his sojourn in Texas. Recognizing a correlation between Huckins's success in his ministry and the financial assistance provided by the society, several members of the congregation asked him to consider requesting reappointment.[14]

The subject was brought before the church at their conference the next week. Huckins indicated he would be willing to be reappointed as a salaried missionary of the American Baptist Home Mission Society if the church felt it appropriate and the society agreed. The church voted to make this request and named Gail Borden to forward the necessary information to the executive committee of the society.[15]

At the same conference, Huckins shared his thoughts regarding the future of the church, especially his conviction that its future success would depend strongly on physical facilities. He then proposed that a concerted effort be made in the United States to raise money to construct a permanent meeting house. The members readily accepted his idea and asked him to be the one to visit the Baptists in the South and East to solicit funds for the project.

Huckins was willing to make the sacrifice and journey to the United States in an attempt to raise money, but he felt he could not go unless a suitable person could be located to manage his academy. He believed in the value of his school and wanted its educational activities to continue. His wife, who had just borne their fourth child two days before, was unable to superintend its operation, and he was not willing to allow the academy to founder even for the important purpose of raising funds for a church edifice.[16]

On 25 March 1845, Borden wrote to the executive committee of the American Baptist Home Mission Society and requested them to recommission Huckins. He had written to them two years previously, shortly before Huckins had become a focal point in the slavery controversy, but his request at that time for Huckins's reappointment had become moot upon Huckins's resignation from the society. Borden believed that his position as a vice president of the society might have some influence in the committee's decision to reemploy Huckins, but he felt even more strongly that the growing spiritual needs of Galveston would convince the committee of the value of giving him a new commission.[17]

Unfortunately, neither Borden's influence nor the religious plight of Galveston had the desired effect as the executive committee did not approve the request. Whether the committee's action was influenced by the continuing controversies between Northern and Southern Baptists, or by some other consideration, is not known.

In spite of the unsuccessful attempt to be reappointed as a missionary, Huckins was convinced that his responsibility as pastor of the Galveston congregation required him to lead in the fund-raising efforts for a permanent meeting house. He therefore decided to make any sacrifices necessary to accomplish this objective.

6

IN JUNE 1845, AFTER finding someone to assume responsibility for the Galveston Academy, Huckins sailed with his family for New York.[1] That same month Gail Borden wrote to the Board of Domestic Missions of the Southern Baptist Convention to explain Huckins's mission and to request financial support for him.[2] This board had been founded a few weeks earlier, at the time of the creation of the Southern Baptist Convention, and as yet had no funds in its treasury. It was therefore unable to lend assistance, but did place Huckins in line for possible consideration in the future.

Upon arriving in Buffalo, Huckins left Rhoda and their children with relatives and began his fund-raising adventures. He took trains and stagecoaches on his longer trips and rented a horse and carriage for the shorter journeys. At associational gatherings, state conventions, church meetings, and special conferences, Huckins discussed the needs of Baptists in Texas, especially his fledgling church in Galveston. From the offerings he received, he deducted fifty dollars per month as his salary plus the amounts necessary to pay his expenses.

During his travels he regularly wrote to Borden and others in Galveston to keep them informed of his progress. From Savannah, Georgia, in December, he sent $438 to Borden for the building fund and indicated that he planned to send more money in two weeks.[3] However, for the next three months not a word was heard from Huckins by anyone in Texas. On 22 March 1846, fearing that Huckins may have died, Borden wrote to the Reverend Basil Manly, former president of the Board of Domestic Missions, and asked for any information which he might have on Huckins's location.[4]

A few days later Borden received a letter from Huckins that had been written previous to the communication to Manly. His failure to write, he explained, had been due to his extremely busy schedule.[5] Earlier in March Huckins had met with the executive committee of the Georgia Baptist Convention in an attempt to gain an endorsement for his work in the state. Not only did the committee recommend his fund-raising mission to the churches of the state convention, but they also sent to the Board of Domestic Missions a proposal relating to the appointment of both Huckins and Tryon as missionaries of that body to Texas. Tryon, pastor of the Houston Baptist Church since the beginning of 1846, had allowed his commission with the American Baptist Home Mission Society to expire in February and had not sought reappointment. Huckins, of course, had resigned his commission in mid-1843. The members of the Georgia Baptist executive committee assured the directors of the mission board that funds for the salaries of Huckins and Tryon would be forthcoming, because of their "conviction that the brethren in Georgia will contribute liberally toward that object."[6]

Shortly after receiving Huckins's letter, Borden and the other members of the Galveston church decided to become more personally involved in the fund-raising activities. The church had thirty-five members at that time—seven white men, nine white women, eleven black women, and eight black men, only one of whom was a free man. From this group, four men and two women were selected to form a committee to "solicit subscriptions to aid in building a Baptist church in this city."[7]

To generate community interest, the church decided to reconstitute its Sabbath school, which had disbanded when the congregation had ceased holding regular meetings in late 1843. For this purpose they rented the lower floor of Joseph Smith's school, where the church was then holding its worship services.[8] They also scheduled prayer meetings for Sunday and Friday nights and set aside Wednesday evenings for the conducting of business. They further hoped to hold worship services whenever possible.[9]

In May, Huckins participated in the twenty-fifth anniversary of the Georgia Baptist Convention and was appointed a delegate from that body to the Southern Baptist Convention to be held in Richmond the next month. At this first gathering of the delegates of the Southern Baptist Convention since its official establishment the previous year, the major theme was missions, both foreign and domestic. Throughout the week, the convention's responsibilities and opportunities in these areas were addressed by numerous speakers, among whom was James Huckins, who discussed the Baptist work in Texas.[10]

During one of the business sessions of the convention, Huckins was named to the Committee on New Fields of Labor, and at another it was announced that he, Tryon, and four others had become the first missionaries to be appointed by the Board of Domestic Missions.[11] Since its creation, the Mission Board had experienced administrative and financial difficulties. Its president, Basil Manly, had resigned soon after accepting the office, and his resignation was quickly followed by that of the secretary. The treasurer then resigned because he was convinced Baptists preferred to conduct mission work through associations and state conventions rather than through a single administrative board.[12] He may have been correct at first, but gradually Baptists across the South began to see advantages in both local and national mission societies, and financial support began to improve. With this increase in available funds and the promise of the Georgia Baptist executive committee for future support, it was anticipated that enough money would be available to fund six missionaries for the next twelve months—one each in Virginia, Florida, Alabama, and Louisiana, and two—Huckins and Tryon—in Texas.

SOON AFTER THE CONVENTION CLOSED, Huckins boarded a ship for New Orleans on his way back to Texas. He had been gone from Galveston an entire year and was anxious to return. Because of illness in his family, he had decided to journey alone, with his wife and daughters to join him at a later date.

Huckins's solicitations in the United States during his twelve-month effort had grossed more than $3,100 in cash plus some $400 in subscriptions. From this amount he had deducted $525 as his salary for ten and a half months, and approximately

$500 for his travel expenses. The time that he had spent with his family resting in New England was not charged against the church.[13]

On board the ship with him were American troops on their way to fight in the war that had recently been declared between the United States and Mexico, a war that had been the inevitable culmination of the Mexican-Texas relationship. While other countries had recognized Texas as an independent member of the family of nations, Mexico had refused to accept the fact. For more than nine years, she had kept alive a threat of hostilities, even making occasional military excursions into Texas. When the United States officially offered to annex the republic in March 1845, the sound of the Mexican war drums beating out their displeasure could be heard from Mexico City to Washington, D.C. Thus when Texas voted to accept annexation a few months later, the United States acquired not only a new state of the Union, but also a "state of smouldering war" with Mexico.[14]

During the interval between the United States' offer and its acceptance by Texas, General Zachary Taylor had been ordered to move his troops, then stationed in western Louisiana, toward the Rio Grande. By October 1845, nearly four thousand U.S. soldiers were camped at the settlement of Corpus Christi, though probably none believed they would ever actually engage in combat with the Mexicans.

Through the fall and winter diplomatic measures sought to resolve the differences between the United States and Mexico, but these attempts only aggravated the situation and caused the two nations to drift slowly toward war. Although most people in the United States probably felt that the problems would never lead to actual combat, preparations were made in event of that possibility.

In late April 1846, a small group of American cavalry was attacked and defeated by a much larger Mexican force on the north bank of the Rio Grande. Within three weeks the United States Congress declared war on Mexico. American soldiers—both regulars and volunteers—soon filled most vessels bound for New Orleans, which rapidly became the major port of embarkation for the war effort. The ship that carried Huckins from the east coast was one of these. In addition to the soldiers on board there were "nearly four hundred sheep on the lower deck, besides pigs and chickens and turkeys on the upper deck."[15] Such crowded and unsanitary conditions made Huckins's two-week trip most unpleasant, especially since he was sick most of the voyage. By the time he arrived in New Orleans on 9 July, he was extremely ill and running a high fever. Deep mental anguish added to his physical discomfort when he found no letters from his wife waiting for him.

While recuperating for two days, Huckins wrote Rhoda, expressing regret at not having received any word from her. He said,

> Had I not been schooled in this kind of disappointment, I should have been sick at heart. I leave in two hours and probably shall not hear from you for a month. What that month may bring forth God only knows. But the will of the Lord be done.[16]

For the past several weeks Huckins had sought comfort through long hours of Bible reading "with peculiar interest and with deep repentance" and in his letter he shared this with Rhoda. He also expressed his concern for their daughter Caroline, who was almost thirteen, asking his wife to "unite with me in fervent prayer, for her speedy conversion." With his letter he forwarded one hundred dollars and promised to send more money soon to pay the doctor's bill.[17]

On 11 July, he boarded the *Galveston* and sailed for his adopted homeland. When he had first seen Texas in 1840, it had been but an infant republic. His departure on his fund-raising expedition in June 1845 had been from a young nation that, while struggling, looked toward a promising future. Now, on his return, Texas was the newest member of the United States and was engaged in a war with her southern neighbor.

The usual three-day trip from New Orleans to Galveston turned into a much longer journey. This ship, like the one on which he arrived in New Orleans, was filled with soldiers who had to be transported to camps near the Rio Grande before any regularly scheduled stops could be made. As a result, Huckins was compelled to endure the tedium and hardships of nearly two additional weeks on the sea before he would finally reach Galveston. For him the time probably passed slowly, because he was eager to get started in the pastorate again.

A few days after Huckins's arrival, the Galveston congregation gathered to hear about his travels and to accept the monies he had collected.[18] They appointed a committee to examine Huckins's records, and two weeks later this committee presented its findings along with resolutions commending Huckins's "sacrifices and self denial" and "his diligent labors."[19]

With reassured faith in the future, the church then selected a building committee, approved the purchase of three lots on which to construct the new sanctuary, and agreed to lease the Galveston Lyceum building for worship services for a period of six months.[20] It was a new beginning for the Galveston Baptist Church.

7

WHEN THE BOARD OF DOMESTIC MISSIONS of the Southern Baptist Convention had commissioned Huckins in the spring of 1846, they had requested him to spend his first months back in Texas traveling over the state to select the most suitable locations for future missionaries. Huckins agreed to this plan, but after returning and seeing the excitement in his congregation, he decided it was more important to remain in Galveston for the next few weeks and make trips to the other locations later.[1]

About two months later he reported to the Mission Board that his

> members have been improving in their religious feelings; take their places in the prayer meetings and Sabbath school—fill their places in the house of God—and begin to feel their responsibilities to God and to the world. I believe the church is united; I know of not the least dissension.[2]

Because of these favorable conditions, Huckins felt he could leave Galveston to attend to other responsibilities, and thus, during the last week of September, he left the city to participate in the Union Baptist Association meeting, scheduled to begin on 1 October 1846, at the Dove church in Caldwell. At this conference the Reverend Hosea Garrett was elected moderator and William Tryon corresponding secretary. For the first time since Tryon had been in Texas he was not chosen moderator.[3]

Huckins, once again, was chosen to preach the introductory sermon for the ensuing year and also was requested to write the Corresponding Letter to the Sabine Baptist Association, which had been organized in northeast Texas in 1843. In addition, he was appointed to the Committee on Union Meetings. That committee recommended that the association be divided into four districts and that each district hold one meeting a year, in addition to the annual gathering of the entire association. After the delegates had accepted this proposal, Huckins volunteered to attend the April meeting of District 2 and the July meeting of District 4. These districts encompassed areas in which Huckins had previously ministered. Several others also volunteered to participate in selected district meetings.[4]

On Sunday, 4 October, Tryon delivered the associational sermon in which he briefly traced the history of the Baptist denomination, including the activities in Texas since 1836. Huckins was so impressed with Tryon's sermon that he recommended it be printed and published with the minutes of the association.[5] The other delegates voiced approval and it was so ordered.

FOLLOWING THIS CONFERENCE, Huckins went to Independence to participate in the meeting of the Baylor University trustees. It was the seventh session of that body, but only the first Huckins had been able to attend. In addition to his own vote, he carried with him the proxy of trustee Eli Mercer, father-in-law of Gail Borden.

Proxies were common in those days of slower communication and transportation, and at previous meetings absent trustees had allowed others to vote for them in this manner. Trustees were not required to designate a proxy, and Huckins had never done so, even though he had missed the first six meetings. Only James L. Farquahar, E. W. Taylor, and J. G. Thomas had attended all the trustee sessions since the first one on 15 May 1845.

At the conference of 8 October 1846, Taylor and Thomas were again present, along with Huckins, Tryon, and A. G. Haynes. Although only five trustees answered the roll, Tryon served as proxy for Robert Armistead, and Haynes for Nelson Kavanaugh. Thus, counting Huckins's proxy for Mercer, eight members were represented, constituting a quorum.[6]

At this meeting Huckins and Tryon were named to a committee to select books for the university, then operating in Independence only a preparatory school with approximately seventy students. The students were meeting in a two-story frame structure on Academy Hill, which had originally housed a school for girls.[7] That school had been established by Frances Trask, a 28-year-old single woman from Massachusetts, in late 1834 and was probably the first of its kind in Texas.[8]

In 1834, Independence, still known by its original name of Coles Settlement, was a very sparsely settled farming community. It had been established by John P. Coles in 1824 and was not organized into a town until 1835. Soon after the signing of the Texas Declaration of Independence on 2 March 1836, the community's name was patriotically changed to Independence.

Miss Trask's school was on one of the several hills which the townsite encompassed. Her facilities included one frame building about fifteen by twenty feet, "with two glazed windows on a side, and folding doors on each end," and a rugged log structure that served for kitchen and storage purposes. She taught at her school until the Revolution in 1836 scattered the families across the country.[9]

About a year after the Republic of Texas was constituted, the Congress chartered an "Independence Academy."[10] That academy probably occupied the same facilities originally owned by Miss Trask, to which a second story was subsequently added. Although the actual starting date of the academy is not known, by May 1839 more than fifty students were enrolled in it.[11]

In 1845 the institution closed and the building was purchased at a sheriff's auction by Independence businessman E. W. Taylor.[12] In the fall of that year, when the Baylor trustees were accepting bids from locations desiring to become the home of the new institution, this facility was a part of the petition of Independence and helped influence the decision of the board in favor of that town. The total value of Independence's bid was more than $2,500 higher than the next highest bid which had been submitted by the town of Huntsville. Other sites considered for the possible location of the university had been Shannon's Prairie and Travis.[13]

After the selection of Independence as the future location of the school, the trustees had to decide which of the properties offered in Independence would make the best location. They first decided to construct a stone facility on Allen Hill, one of the other properties included in the bid, since this site was less than three miles from an excellent quarry, which could furnish the necessary materials for the building. However, at a meeting on 12 January 1846, after looking into the cost of erecting such a stone structure, the trustees decided instead to repair the former Independence Academy building and temporarily delay further construction. They believed that in this way they might save money, of which they had very little, and also advance the opening date of the school.[14] The trustees then, in order to assist with future building projects and help guarantee operational expenses, appointed agents to solicit funds both in Texas and in the United States. In additional business they elected Henry Lee Graves as president and Henry Flavel Gillett as teacher in the preparatory school.

An 1833 honor graduate of the University of North Carolina at the age of twenty, Graves's first teaching assignment had been at Wake Forest College. He had married in 1836 and moved to Cave Springs, Georgia, the following year to head a Baptist high school. From 1840 to 1842 he had studied at the Hamilton Literary and Theological Institute at Hamilton, New York, and since that time had been teaching school in Covington, Georgia.[15]

Gillett, an active member of the Episcopal church, was teaching in the Houston Academy which he and his uncle, the Reverend Charles Gillett, an Episcopalian minister, had established in 1844. Well known to many of the trustees and a close friend of several leading Texas governmental officials, Henry Gillett had come to Texas in 1839 and operated a small school in Houston for two years. In the summer of 1841 he moved to Washington County to open Union Academy, about three miles from Washington-on-the-Brazos, teaching there until early 1843, when he turned to farming. While at Union Academy he boarded at the home of James Farquahar for a time, and when he was married on 3 March, 1842, William Tryon performed the ceremony. Both Farquahar and Tryon were on the original trustee board of the university. Gillett returned to teaching in Houston after farming about a year.[16]

The Baylor preparatory department opened under Gillett's supervision on 18 May 1846. However, Graves had still not assumed his responsibilities when the trustees gathered for the 8 October meeting. At this session Huckins presented a plan for alternating the responsibility for leadership in Sunday worship services at the school. This proposal, which received the wholehearted support of the other trustees, called for Baptists to conduct the services on the first Sunday in every month, Methodists on the second, and Presbyterians on the fourth. The third Sunday was to be left open to "any Christian denomination."[17]

After the trustee meeting, Huckins spent the next several weeks surveying the spiritual conditions in communities located between the Brazos and Trinity rivers in order to recommend intelligently appropriate mission stations for the three missionaries whom the Board of Domestic Missions had recently appointed to serve in Texas. He then went to Houston and stayed with Tryon for several days before returning to Galveston.[18]

By mid-November, plans for the new Galveston church structure had been completed and all contracts signed. Construction, however, was delayed, because most of the ships coming to Galveston still were being used for the war effort. Consequently, they had little room available in them to carry materials for civilian building projects.

Huckins used this period of time to lead the fund-raising efforts that several members in the church had initiated that spring. The proposed church building was expected to cost nearly five thousand dollars, and more money was needed to assure its completion. He soon obtained eight hundred dollars from Galveston citizens, and Huckins felt he could collect seven hundred dollars more in the near future.

Because of his love and concern for the Galveston congregation, Huckins expended a great amount of energy toward assisting them in their spiritual growth, a task which met with great success during the fall and early winter of 1846. By the end of November, less than five months after Huckins's return from the

United States, the Galveston church had added fourteen members by letter and two by baptism. Though the church work required a lot of his time, Huckins made it a point to visit regularly those in the hospitals, and even established a preaching station at Bolivar Point, a small settlement just a few miles from Galveston.[19]

Although Huckins was pleased with the success he was witnessing in his personal ministry, he was, perhaps, even more pleased to observe the results of the joint venture in which he and the other evangelical ministers were participating. For several weeks these men had been holding weekly meetings for prayer and "for devising modes of attack upon the bulwarks of Satan." The Christian atmosphere being manifested in the city appeared to be directly linked to these efforts.[20]

Another pleasant occurrence for Huckins took place during the first week of December, when he had the opportunity to welcome to Texas four Baptist ministers. Three of them, Noah Hill, P. B. Chandler, and J. W. D. Creath, were the newly appointed Southern Baptist missionaries for whom he had been making preparations. The other was Henry L. Graves, president-elect of Baylor University.

In recounting his feelings in a report to the Board of Domestic Missions shortly after their arrival, he said,

> It was a glorious day to my own soul, and which opens a new era to the denomination in Texas. The spirit of these missionaries, the profound sense of the nature and responsibility of their work, the hours of agonizing prayer during their passage, made me feel, during my interview with them, that I was in the company of holy men; men called of God to come to Texas.[21]

These new "Texans" had journeyed together from New Orleans. Hill, Chandler, and Graves had shared company since leaving Georgia in November, traveling overland to Montgomery, Alabama, where they took a ship to New Orleans. There they had met Creath who had come from Virginia by water. Creath had decided to become a missionary to Texas during the

Southern Baptist Convention at which Huckins had made an appeal for volunteers.[22]

After a brief stay in Galveston and another in Houston to visit Tryon, Creath went to Montgomery County to begin his labors, and Chandler took up his ministry in Fayette County. Hill was assigned to Matagorda, Brazoria, and Wharton counties.

Graves remained at the home of Gail Borden for a short time. Then, loading his family, servants, household goods, and furnishings into the wagons that he had brought with him on the ship, he journeyed to Independence to assume his new post. Though now a major stagecoach stop between Houston and Austin, Independence was still a primitive town. However, its future looked promising, as the educational opportunities at Baylor had begun to lure people to settle nearby.

8

IN JANUARY 1847, though the war with Mexico was still being waged, requirements for troops were not as great as before. Thus ships had more space available for supplies. As a result, by the middle of the month the milled lumber that had been ordered by the Galveston church arrived, enabling construction to begin on the new worship center. This seemed to spark a feeling of enthusiasm among the members. The weekly prayer meetings became crowded again, and eleven people applied for membership.

In spite of this success, Huckins was not entirely pleased with his ministry. He was having difficulty convincing some Christians who had not yet joined any church in the city of their responsibilities and the need for "prompt, regular and conscientious cooperation with the pastor in all his labors of love."[1] Though he was not successful in leading all such persons back into active work for the Lord, he continually tried, seeking them out and not giving "them up until they fill their place in the church."[2]

In a report to the Board of Domestic Missions, Huckins indicated the success he was having with these people, noting that

> Several of this number are now rejoicing in the possession of a religious home with us, which they begin to love; while others of these are beginning to loiter around the fold of Christ, awaiting the opportunity of entering.[3]

This same report to the board was filled with Huckins's pleadings for pastors and churches in the older states to impress upon their members the need of joining a sister church as soon as possible after relocating to a new community. Huckins believed that if this were done "many cases of apostacy might be saved, and our young and feeble churches in the new states would be relieved of a most grievous embarrassment."[4]

Not only was the Galveston church experiencing a religious renewal in the early weeks of 1847, but the Houston Baptist Church also was growing in numbers and spirit. Tryon reported to the board that there were "indications of seriousness in our congregation, which are quite encouraging."[5]

The building programs of these churches—Houston being slightly ahead of Galveston—encouraged other communities to emulate them. One of these was Lynchburg, a small town twenty-five miles south of Houston on the bayou leading to Galveston Bay, in which the citizens built a "house of worship, to be occupied by four denominations, Baptists, Presbyterians, Methodists and Roman Catholics."[6] The people of Lynchburg anticipated that Huckins and Tryon would share the responsibility of filling the pulpit on the Sundays available to the Baptists.

By May the new building of the Houston church was completed, and Huckins and Baylor president Henry L. Graves assisted Tryon in the dedication service. This occasion might have encouraged the Galveston congregation to complete rapidly its facility, but as summer approached the Galveston congregation seemed to experience a spiritual relapse. Huckins attributed this to several factors, including the intense heat and the vacationing of the members, but he also felt that he might be partly to blame.

Because of the added responsibilities of superintending the building of the new meeting house, he had not had sufficient time to visit regularly the members or to adequately prepare his sermons. In spite of the fact that there was a church-elected building committee, most of the work relating to the construction of the new facility fell upon his shoulders. The added responsibility took more of his time than he felt best for the total good of the church.[7]

Though several members of the Galveston church were absent from the weekly worship activities during the early summer, the fruits of Huckins's labor in the United States more than a year before continued to deliver dividends. Letters filled with encouragement and donations frequently arrived to provide a special spiritual as well as financial uplift to Huckins and to his ministry. In late July Huckins wrote the editor of the *Christian Index* to express his gratitude to the many people in Georgia who had made the contributions. He indicated that both the money and the encouragement "came in the right time for my heart was sad and my pockets were empty."[8]

An especially happy occasion for Huckins during the summer was the opportunity to baptize an eighty-seven-year-old woman. Unable to walk to the shores of the Gulf of Mexico to be immersed, she was carried by three men. The service was very emotional to the onlookers. Huckins later said of the elderly lady that,

> Though very weak and infirm, yet she bore it with all the firmness of a woman of strength. On being borne out of the water, her countenance beamed with almost heavenly light, and seemed to indicate emotions similar to those which swelled the bosoms of good old Simeon and Anna. It was enough—they had seen Christ. It was enough—she had followed Christ, and was ready to die in peace whenever her Master should call for her.[9]

On 2 July 1847, the Galveston Baptist Church met in a business session at the Galveston Lyceum to discuss the pastor's salary and to formulate plans for renting the pews in the meeting house, which was nearing completion. Huckins had received only three hundred dollars since his resumption of the pastorate following his return from the year-long fund-raising trip in the South and East. Therefore, a committee was appointed to raise immediately the remaining two hundred dollars owed him.

At this meeting the members voted to recall Huckins as their pastor for the next year at an annual salary of five hundred dollars. Combined with the money that he was receiving from the Board of Domestic Missions, they felt this salary would adequately meet his needs.[10] Huckins accepted the church's call. But he informed the members that since he also was employed by the Southern Baptist Convention, he would have to share some of his time with other congregations in the interior of the state, and probably take frequent excursions to establish mission stations. These conditions were accepted by the members of the church.[11]

As construction of the church building was nearing completion, Huckins had more time to devote to that part of the ministry that he loved—leading people to Christ. Within a short time he baptized several people and had others preparing for the ordinance. Prospects seemed bright, but there was a rumbling in the church, an undercurrent caused by the dissatisfaction of some members with the pastor.

Even though Huckins's election to serve the church for another year had been unanimous, the deacons felt that there was a lack of sincerity on the part of several members. Thus, soon after the meeting, they began to poll the members individually about their real feelings toward Huckins. Unaware of dissension, Huckins wrote to the Board of Domestic Missions that everything about the church was promising and that "his heart and hands are full of labor," indicating that in about six weeks construction on the new facility would be completed.[12]

ON 12 SEPTEMBER 1847, the day for which the Galveston congregation had long waited, dedication ceremonies for the new church building were held. Unfortunately, Huckins, who had spent a year in the eastern states raising money, and who had given so much time and energy seeking contributions locally, as well as directing all the constructional activities, was unable to participate due to illness. To lead the service, William Tryon came from Houston and was assisted by the pastors of the local German Methodist Episcopal Church and the Presbyterian Church.[13]

The following week, evidence of discontent became known to Huckins when he received a letter from the deacons requesting his resignation. The major reason given for the request related to "prejudices" held by some of the members against Huckins, specifically several couples with young children. Although the nature of the prejudices was not given, the letter stated that they were "so great that it is with difficulty they [the children] can be persuaded to attend Divine service." The deacons were satisfied that Huckins had always "manifested a great desire for the conversion of our children, but this cannot be effected in the absence of attachment for the minister."[14]

Though not certain whether the prejudices were "well or ill founded" or whether they could be solved, the deacons perceived the current situation as "lamentable." They felt that the only solution was for Huckins to resign. No other charges were specified, but the letter did indicate that the church leaders had knowledge of several people in the city who also were prejudiced against Huckins. In requesting his resignation, the deacons did express regret "in consideration of your having so perseveringly and assiduously laboured in the erection of our House of Worship."[15]

Huckins abided by the petition of the deacons and on 26 September sent a letter of resignation before the church in which he stated that his "labor as minister of the gospel in this city will close in three months from this day." He also said,

> In the interval between this and my final separation from the congregation with the leave of God, I will supply the pulpit, perform the labors of pastor, give my attention to settling up the pecuniary affairs of the church, and aid you in any consistent way toward procuring you another minister.[16]

Huckins did not want his departure to be a divisive factor in the church, and so he added,

> Let me have the privilege of visiting your families as I have been accustomed to do, without references being made to the causes which have led to this step; for such conversation could answer no good purpose.[17]

He stressed that he still loved the church members and that his prayers and best wishes would always be with them. He closed his letter with the admonition to the members to act wisely before God and man "and do nothing which will cause you regret in the last hours of life; or which shall be offensive to Him, before whom you and I must shortly appear."[18]

When the congregation met to receive Huckins's resignation on 6 October, sixteen members were present. Only one voted negatively, so his resignation was accepted. To express their appreciation of the pastor's services, the group then adopted a resolution which stated

> That the warmest thanks of the members of this church be returned to Brother Huckins for his untiring energy and perseverance in obtaining and collecting subscriptions for our new place of worship; confidently believing that had it not been for the zeal exhibited by him we would have been compelled to content ourselves with a far inferior building.[19]

A few days after his resignation, Huckins went to Houston to participate in the eighth annual meeting of the Union Baptist Association. He was supposed to preach the introductory sermon, but did not arrive in time, so J. W. D. Creath substituted for him.

The delegates from the twenty churches which gathered for this five-day conference included the new Southern Baptist missionaries and many of the trustees of Baylor University. It was here that the ministers and laymen learned of Huckins's resignation. It was probably the first forced resignation in the association since Cox was expunged in 1841.

At the meeting Tryon was once again elected moderator. J. G. Thomas was reelected clerk, and Henry L. Graves was chosen corresponding secretary. In this capacity Graves was requested to correspond with the other associations and individual churches across the state to ascertain interest in forming a general convention.

Although some people in Galveston held "prejudices" against Huckins, there was no indication of such in the associational gathering. The representatives of the churches respected him so that, when five churches requested permission to withdraw from the Union Association to form their own group, Huckins was the first person selected to assist in the constitution of this new association. He also was named to the committee to oversee the 1848 union meetings.

During the Saturday recess in the associational activities, those present who also were members of the Texas Baptist Education Society held their annual meeting. At this gathering the society took an offering of more than three hundred dollars and admitted twenty-three new members into the group.[20] Individuals could become members of the society simply by verifying with their signatures acceptance of its constitution. Non-Baptists could be active members, but only those "in communion with some regular Baptist church" could be on the executive committee.[21]

At this meeting, Huckins presented four resolutions, all of which were adopted. The first stressed the need to pray for more ministers to come to Texas, and the second emphasized the importance of developing more ministers from within the state itself. Directly related to the second resolution were the remaining two: an appeal for a systematic effort to "be made to assist young men of piety and promise in their preparation for the ministry," and the statement that Baylor University was the most logical place "to carry out the designs of this society."[22]

In the circular letter of the association, Huckins's concern for better prepared ministers was reinforced. The author, William Tryon, discussed the need of churches to support their pastors on a full-time basis, thereby freeing them from secular work. This would, Tryon indicated, allow more time for study and enable the pastors to become more "skillful builders in Christ's spiritual temple."[23]

During the rest of the year Huckins devoted much of his attention to the needs of the general population of Galveston. Several of the leaders of the public school system had resigned that fall, and Huckins volunteered to serve without pay as the head instructor so that the children of the city could continue their education.[24] In addition, because of the rapid spread of yellow fever through the Gulf communities, Huckins was called upon constantly to assist the sick, the dying, the dead, and the bereaved—a ministry in which he excelled.

One of the victims felled during the epidemic was William Tryon. Although many in Houston had retreated northward in an effort to escape the disease, Tryon had remained to assist those in need. During the first week of November he had contracted the fever, lingering only ten days before he passed away. His ministry in Texas had lasted less than seven years, but it had been a most effective one. He was mourned by his friends throughout the entire Baptist denomination.[25]

IN HUCKINS'S FINAL 1847 REPORT to the Board of Domestic Missions, he expressed continued interest in the spiritual welfare of the people of Texas. In spite of his personal sacrifices and the calamities through which he had led so many people, he remained optimistic about the future of the state and especially of the Baptist denomination. He praised God for leading him westward and expressed gratitude for the many opportunities he had had to share Christ's love in Texas. He was pleased to have been able to encourage so many ministers to come to Texas to serve the Lord.[26]

On 22 December, just a few days before Huckins's resignation as pastor of the Galveston Baptist Church was to become effective, the Baylor University Board of Trustees voted to employ him as agent of the institution at an annual salary of one thousand dollars.[27] The appointment of Huckins as an agent for the institution was not the first such appointment made by the trustees. In fact, almost since the establishment of the school, agents had been serving to collect money, land, and subscriptions. J. M. Norris was the first, having been employed to secure titles to specific lands included in Independence's gift to Baylor.

In January 1846, when the trustees had requested Henry Lee Graves to become president of the university, they also had asked him to serve as agent in Georgia while preparing to move to Texas. At that same meeting the board had named Richard Ellis as domestic agent and Stephen F. Adams as agent in Mississippi. They also had called upon R. E. B. Baylor and William Tryon to serve as both domestic and foreign agents.[28] Approximately a year later the trustees requested Rufus C. Burleson, then a student at Western Baptist Theological Seminary in Covington, Kentucky, to solicit contributions in Kentucky, Ohio, Mississippi, and Alabama, promising him 10 percent of the amount collected.[29] During most of 1847 the university also had several volunteer agents attempting to secure contributions. Huckins, along with three other trustees and several missionaries, were among this group.[30] The difference in Huckins's current appointment and those previously made by the trustees was that this was the first time an agent had been named for a specific period of time at a designated salary.

The trustees were not seeking to employ Huckins simply because he had lost his church position. He probably was the most experienced fund-raiser in the state and was well known in Texas and across the United States. They felt his knowledge, contacts, and experience would be invaluable and prove extremely advantageous in securing donations for the university's needs.

The Baylor board was not the only group interested in Huckins's fund-raising abilities. The Southern Baptist Convention's Board of Domestic Missions wanted to change his "missionary" status to "agent" and to employ him to canvass Texas on their behalf. Though it was a unique opportunity, he declined the mission board's offer and accepted the cause of Christian education at Baylor.

In order to serve the university on a full-time basis, Huckins resigned as a missionary of the Southern Baptist Convention. However, he agreed to spend January and February 1848 preaching in churches in Galveston and in Washington and Burleson counties as his final obligations.

9

IN MARCH 1848, AS HUCKINS BEGAN work for Baylor, the future of Texas looked very bright. The war with Mexico had concluded with a resounding American triumph that would eventually add more than 525,000 square miles to the western territory of the United States. Immigration was continuing into the state, raising the population to more than 140,000.[1] The economy was improving and interest in education was growing, with several private academies and universities having been recently established.

In addition to the favorable outlook for the general condition of the state, the prospects for the Baptist denomination also appeared quite favorable. Several new churches had been established, the Colorado and Soda Lake associations had been organized, the Southern Baptist Board of Domestic Missions had appointed more missionaries to the state, and church members throughout the South were giving generously to support the Christian causes in Texas. It seemed a most propitious time for Huckins to start his new "calling."

When the Baylor trustees met in June, Huckins made his first report. Although there is no record of the amount of money he had collected during his first three months, evidently he had not raised much, because he and ten other trustees had to contribute from their personal funds to pay that which was due on the previous year's salaries of President Henry L. Graves and Professor H. F. Gillett.[2]

At this meeting the board expressed its appreciation to Gillett, whose term of employment had just concluded with the close of the spring session, for "the able and satisfactory" manner in which he had conducted the preparatory school since its establishment in May 1846.[3] Since Gillett was not reemployed, the trustees authorized Graves to manage both the collegiate and preparatory departments and to employ the teachers. To pay the salaries and expenses, Graves was to receive all monies collected for tuition and fees.

Also during this session, the trustees reconfirmed their intention to build a two-story stone structure on Allen Hill for the preparatory department, instructing Huckins to secure appropriate titles to the land from the donors as soon as possible. They then named Huckins and J. R. Hines, a layman serving as proxy at the meeting for R. E. B. Baylor, as a committee to supervise the construction of this building, which was to measure fifty-five by thirty-five feet. Following a recess in the proceedings, the board added John McKnight to the committee. McKnight, who operated a drugstore in a stone building on the Independence town square, like Hines, was not a trustee, but it was felt he could provide information "which he may think important."[4] In addition to this action, the trustees, realizing that a master development plan would prove advantageous to any fund-raising efforts, directed Huckins and Hines to develop such a plan for "all the grounds, buildings and improvements contemplated by the Board."[5]

Because of constitutional provisions prohibiting a trustee from being an employee of the university, Huckins was required to resign from the board, which he did on the third and last day of this June meeting. He was the fourth of the original trustees to leave the board—E. W. Taylor had resigned the day before; Robert Armistead had relinquished his position at a previous meeting; and Tryon had died in November 1847. Hines was immediately appointed to take Huckins's place.

For the next several months Huckins worked in the areas of the state being served by the Southern Baptist missionaries, preaching in their churches and encouraging the listeners to contribute to Baylor. In many of these places he had pioneered the Baptist work. Thus he enjoyed seeing the progress that was being made and the reception the people were giving to the Gospel. Although his major focus was on solicitation, his thoughts frequently turned to Galveston and the first church he had organized in Texas. In a special report which he sent to the Board of Domestic Missions during this time, he stated, "My heart bleeds for that church."[6]

On 8 September 1848, Huckins joined fifty-four other delegates from twenty-one Baptist churches to organize the Baptist State Convention. Since leaving the pastorate, he had placed his membership with the Independence church and was a representative of that congregation at the meeting which was held in Antioch Baptist church in Anderson. Henry L. Graves, R. E. B. Baylor, J. H. Stribling, and A. G. Haynes also represented the Independence church. Gail Borden was a delegate from the Galveston church along with its new pastor, J. F. Hillyer.

Huckins was an active participant during this five-day conference, and was named to the education committee and the special committee to draft the constitution. He also was selected the alternate preacher of the convention sermon for the next annual session, and named one of two delegates to the 1849 Southern Baptist Convention. In addition, he was elected a vice president of the body, along with J. W. D. Creath and Hosea Garrett, both current trustees of Baylor University. Creath had replaced E. W. Taylor, and Garrett had been named to take the place of Robert Armistead.

Under the leadership of Huckins, the education committee proposed several resolutions to the convention, all of which were adopted. The resolutions emphasized the importance of "sound learning," stressed the need for contributions and prayer to support Baylor, and recommended that churches take an annual offering to assist "young men in procuring a suitable education, who shall give evidence of being called to preach the gospel."[7]

Two weeks after the convention closed, Huckins went to Independence to attend the annual Union Baptist Association. It was one of the few times he was not on the program to preach the introductory or associational sermon for this group, though he never had actually delivered either. Each time he had been scheduled, he arrived late or failed to make the meeting altogether, and someone had to be called upon to preach for him. J. W. D. Creath was supposed to preach at this ninth anniversary of the association, but when he did not arrive by the appropriate time, Huckins was persuaded to replace him. Thus, ironically, the first sermon Huckins ever delivered before the Union Association was given as a substitute.

Another first for Huckins, and also for the association, occurred when he was elected moderator, the first time that a minister not currently serving as a pastor of a specific congregation was elected to this position. On Thursday evening, during a recess in the associational sessions, the Texas Baptist Education Society met and elected officers. Once again Huckins was honored by being elected treasurer of this organization.[8]

Later that year, in addition to the duties previously assigned him by the convention, the association, and the Education Society, Huckins assumed yet another responsibility, this one from outside the state. The editors of the *South Western Baptist Chronicle,* a weekly newspaper published in New Orleans, chose him to be the Texas agent for their periodical. The *Chronicle* was but one of several Baptist papers published and circulated in the United States, but it was the only one "officially" recommended for Texas Baptists.

Baptists historically had used books and tracts to spread religious news and promote their causes, but by the beginning of the nineteenth century denominationally oriented newspapers had begun to make inroads into the field of communication. The first weekly Baptist newspaper was established in Boston in 1819 and was soon followed by similar publications from Georgia to Maine. By the 1830s, Baptist newspapers were being used to distribute religious information across the nation.

For several years Huckins had used newspapers to promote his work. As an agent of the American Baptist Home Mission Society in Georgia he had used the *Christian Index* to keep the Baptists in that state informed of his traveling schedule. On his first trip to Texas in 1840 he had kept a journal, much of which was later published in the *Index.* During his early travels in the republic he frequently had written personal letters to various Baptist editors, knowing that the contents would probably be published in the pages of their newspapers. In 1841 he served as the editor of a Texas column which sporadically appeared in the Kentucky-based *Baptist Banner and Western Pioneer.*

Since the days of the republic, Baptist periodicals had been cherished reading in Texas. Most were published in the eastern states and, though they carried general as well as religious news from all over the world, they contained little of what the Baptists in Texas really wanted—news about Texas and Baptist activities there. Undependable postal service made delivery of the various journals and newspapers published in the United States irregular, but when they did arrive in Texas they were thoroughly read and frequently shared with friends and neighbors.

When the *South Western Baptist Chronicle* began publication from New Orleans in 1847, its proximity to Texas enabled the editors to gather and include more news about the Lone Star state and to reduce the time interval between publication and delivery. As a result the *Chronicle* soon outstripped all other Baptist publications in readership among Texans.

In the fall of 1847 the Union Association passed a resolution naming the *Chronicle* as the newspaper best suited to serve the needs of Baptists in Texas. When the Baptist State Convention was organized the following year, there was some discussion relating to the propriety of starting a denominational paper in the state. However, opposition quickly arose, resulting in the tabling of the idea and the adoption of the *Chronicle* as the "official" Baptist voice in Texas.

With an opportunity like this to become established in Texas, it was only natural for the editors of the *Chronicle* to choose Huckins, one of the most respected denominational leaders in the state, to represent their paper. They anticipated that he would be able to promote the sale of subscriptions during his extensive travels across Texas.

DURING THE FIRST FEW MONTHS OF 1849 Huckins's routine differed little from the previous year. Again he spent many lonely hours on horseback following poorly marked trails, crossing wild prairies, swimming swollen streams and creeks, and passing through dark forests in an attempt to encourage people to give money to Baylor. He was frequently away from his family for weeks at a time, but he accepted this hardship because he believed in the value of Christian education.

At a called meeting of the Baylor board of trustees in April, Huckins reported a highly successful first year of employment. Since beginning his work in March 1848, he had collected more than $9,600 in cash and subscriptions, including ten thousand acres of land. Because of his own commitment to Baylor, Huckins then tendered to the trustees $403.87—the amount still due on his annual salary, and also offered them a $225 cash loan. The money was accepted, but both gifts were considered loans.[9]

At this meeting the trustees voted to continue Huckins's employment as agent for another year at the same salary. Knowing he would be gone most of the time, they excused him from serving on the building committee to which he had been appointed the previous June. Since John McKnight had been just a temporary member of the building committee, this left only J. R. Hines with the responsibility to oversee the construction of the planned facility. Realizing the amount of work that would be required to supervise this project, the board appointed four more trustees to the building committee.

In May 1849, Huckins participated in the second annual session of the Baptist State Convention. It was held in Houston, but because rumors had spread across the state about an outbreak of cholera in that city, less than thirty delegates came to the convention. One of those who was not present was Baylor president Henry L. Graves, who also was president of the convention. As a result, Huckins, as one of the vice presidents, was called upon to preside at all the sessions.

During this conference, Huckins was reelected a vice president and was named, along with four others, to discuss some of the provisions of Baylor's charter with representatives of the Texas Baptist Education Society. Under consideration was an application to the Texas legislature that would change a part of the university's charter, permitting trustee vacancies to be filled by the convention rather than by the Education Society's executive committee. The representatives from the society and the convention agreed with this plan and recommended that the charter of Baylor University be amended, suggesting that a joint committee present this proposal at the next legislature.[10]

On Sunday, the third day of the meeting, Huckins preached

the convention sermon, in which he focused on the value of giving in the name of Christ. As he usually tried to make the most of every opportunity to raise funds for Baylor, he followed his address by taking an offering for educational purposes.[11]

During the summer, Huckins boarded with J. W. D. Creath in Huntsville and concentrated his work in Polk, Walker, Grimes, and Montgomery counties.[12] In August the Baylor trustees recommended that he embark on a fund-raising expedition through the southern and eastern states. To this end they furnished him credentials certifying the validity of his agency and wrote several Baptist newspaper editors seeking publicity for his mission.[13]

10

IN THE FALL OF 1849 Huckins and his family once again set sail for the east coast. This trip would mark the third time he had left Texas for an extended period to solicit contributions. His first excursion of about six months had been in 1840, after his exploratory visit to the Republic of Texas. The second, when he had sought support for the Galveston Baptist Church, had lasted a full year. This time the trip would be even longer.

Because of the cold and severe winter weather during the last part of 1849 and the early months of 1850, Huckins remained with his family in Providence, Rhode Island, not charging the university for this time since he was not at work on its behalf. As conditions moderated in the spring, he journeyed to the South to begin his work.

In June 1850, Huckins sent drafts totaling six hundred dollars to the Baylor trustees and indicated he would continue as their agent for another year. The trustees approved his reappointment and named A. G. Haynes and R. E. B. Baylor as a committee to correspond with Huckins. They were to "advise him from time to time, relative to such means as they may deem expedient for the advancement of the general interest and well being of the institution."[1]

Throughout the remainder of the year Huckins traveled extensively and spoke to as many church groups as he could schedule. He usually was well received and frequently was commended by Baptist newspaper editors for his efforts. Often he became so involved in his work that he neglected to keep the Baylor trustees informed of his whereabouts, depending instead on notices published about his activities in various Baptist papers to provide that information. It was not the most efficient means of communication, and its effectiveness was completely forfeited if the trustees failed to read a particular publication that mentioned him.

Early the next year he acquired a "set of philosophical and chemical apparatus" in Boston and shipped it to the university. This equipment, some of the first of its kind ever seen in Texas, was used to perform demonstrations before the students and special guests during the spring 1851 commencement exercises.[2] Other than the receipt of this equipment, the trustees had little communication from Huckins during the first five months of the year.

On Friday, 13 June 1851, when the board assembled for its annual session, one of the first orders of business was the appointment of a four-member committee to discuss the propriety of appointing another agent. The committee, composed of R. E. B. Baylor, Aaron Shannon, J. L. Farquahar, and R. B. Jarman, considered the idea, but concluded that the employment of another agent was not necessary. Instead they recommended that Huckins be allowed more time to communicate with the board. This proposal was accepted, but the trustees, anxious to hear from Huckins, instructed the treasurer to try to contact him and ask him to return to Texas "as soon as practicable." The school's stone structure had been completed, and the building committee needed the funds Huckins was collecting to help defray the costs of its construction.[3]

The following day, 14 June, Baylor president Henry L. Graves gave his report on the state of the institution and then unexpectedly offered his resignation.[4] Since taking office in February 1847, Graves had been a very effective leader. During his four years as president, he had led the small, struggling school through a period of unusual financial and scholastic adjustments. He had the entire operational responsibility after H. F. Gillett's term of service ended in 1848 and had been vitally involved in the institution's building program. In addition, he had been a leading figure in the organization of the Baptist State Convention, as well as its first president.

On Monday, 16 June, the trustees accepted Graves's resignation with regret, and then appointed a committee to seek and recommend his successor. That evening the board met with the delegates to the Baptist State Convention, then in session on the Baylor campus. The main address to the assembly was delivered by Texas supreme court associate justice Abner S. Lipscomb, who had been lecturing on law at Baylor on a voluntary basis for the past two years. He gave a moving speech on the need for endowing the presidency of the university, a program that had been initiated in June 1850, but one that had had little success.

The timing of Lipscomb's address was fortunate. There had been a growing recognition among the Baptists in the state regarding the need to establish a sound financial foundation for Baylor, and Graves's unexpected resignation had heightened concern for the institution's future. When Lipscomb finished his message, a special offering was taken and more than fifty-five hundred dollars was subscribed toward a ten-thousand-dollar endowment fund goal. It was the first real outpouring of Baptist support for the institution.[5]

On Tuesday the committee selected to recommend a new president presented the name of twenty-seven-year-old Rufus C. Burleson. He was well known to many of the trustees, since he had served as an agent of the university while a student at Western Baptist Theological Seminary in Kentucky and had been pastor of the Houston First Baptist Church for more than three years.

After completing his seminary education in June 1847, Burleson had applied to the Southern Baptist Convention's Board of Domestic Missions to become a missionary to Texas. He was assigned to the Gonzales area, but before arriving was reappointed to become pastor of the First Baptist Church of Houston to replace William Tryon who had died that November. He was well respected in Texas and had been the corresponding secretary of the Baptist State Convention since its organization in 1848. He was a very popular preacher and spent a lot of time conducting evangelistic services across the state. In fact, because of his interest in evangelism he had resigned his pastorate in September 1850 to work full-time in that field, but the church would not accept his resignation.[6]

The trustees considered Burleson an excellent choice and unanimously elected him the second president of the university, appointing a three-member committee to notify him of his selection. Burleson, who had remained in Independence following the conclusion of the Baptist State Convention, met with the board the next day and accepted the position.

The trustees then elected Horace Clark and his wife, along with Miss Harriet Davis, to take charge of the female department of the institution. Clark, a native of Massachusetts, had received his education in Illinois at Shurtleff College. He had taught in Georgetown College for four years and had headed a private academy in New Castle, Kentucky, from 1846 to 1850, when he moved to Texas to become the president of the La Grange Collegiate Institute. When he learned of the trustees' decision to employ him, he immediately rode horseback from La Grange to Independence to accept. His only condition was that the trustees arrange for the development of proper instructional facilities for the young ladies.[7]

AS THE TRUSTEES BEGAN PLANNING for more appropriate quarters for the female department, and the new faculty and administration prepared to open the next session of the university in August, Huckins was still out of the state on his fundraising assignment. The trustees were becoming very anxious for his return, because the money he had collected, which was still in his possession, was needed to pay for repairs already made to some of the facilities as well as to pay interest due on outstanding loans.

When Huckins had still not returned by the December meeting of the board, the trustees instructed the secretary to request several Baptist newspapers to publish a notification for Huckins to return to Texas as soon as possible. The trustees hoped that Huckins might read the notice and be made aware of their wishes. Following this action the trustees employed J. W. D. Creath to "collect funds and raise subscriptions for the Baylor University for the term of three months from this time or until Br. Huckins returns."[8]

Trustee secretary George W. Baines wrote letters on behalf

of the board on 15 December and mailed them to Baptist papers in Georgia, Alabama, and New York. Huckins probably never saw any of the papers that carried the trustees' plea, for he was already on the way back to Texas by the time the trustees' communication could have reached the editors.[9]

When Huckins arrived in Independence on 10 January 1852, he had with him more than sixty-four hundred dollars, including a personal donation of his own. In addition, he had about five hundred dollars worth of books and pledges for some nine hundred dollars. Of the total amount collected, thirteen hundred dollars was designated to endow the presidency.

At the trustee meeting later that month, Huckins discussed his travels and presented the funds he had collected. The board adopted a resolution of appreciation to him "for his liberal favors bestowed on Baylor University and for efficient services as agent for the same." They then readily voted to reemploy him for the year 1852.[10] Huckins, however, did not as readily accept their offer. He had been raising money for the institution for almost four years, and though he realized the importance of his work, his real interest lay in the pastoral ministry to which he wanted to return.

During the time he had been in the South and East, Huckins had not only shared the needs of Baylor with Baptist audiences, but had also carefully observed the spiritual needs of the areas in which he visited. One of the main needs he noticed was for more pastors to fill the numerous vacant pulpits.

For several years the Board of Domestic Missions had advocated an annual increase of five hundred ministers to meet the vacancies that existed in the Baptist churches.[11] The disparity between the number of vacant pulpits and the ministers available to fill them deeply disturbed Huckins as he traveled from state to state. In a letter to a friend about the matter, he stated that "My heart pants for retirement [from agency work] and for the regular duties of the humble minister of Jesus Christ."[12]

He told him,

> The cry for faithful ministers of Christ begins again to ring in my ears, and to pain my soul. How can this cry

be met unless God in mercy shall raise up more laborers. O that a spirit of importunate prayer could be awakened amongst our churches, that God would raise up and send forth into this mighty field such men as he will own and bless.[13]

Although Huckins preferred to be just a "humble minister" and fill an empty pulpit somewhere in Texas, that opportunity was not made available at this time. He therefore agreed to serve as agent for the university for another year. However, because of certain convictions, he placed several stipulations on his acceptance.

Huckins felt that the financial management of the university had not been efficient and that the best principles of business practice were not being followed. To help alleviate this situation he requested the trustees to agree to make no further appropriations until all liabilities of the school were liquidated. He felt an obligation to the donors "who look to me in some degree for the judicious expenditure of their money" and therefore asked the board to assure that the money received would be used as specified by its contributors.[14] Because of his personal observations of the quality of buildings and equipment at many of the eastern educational institutions and because of his belief that the quality of facilities was directly related to the quality of education which they fostered, Huckins also requested that the trustees pledge to attempt to build better educational and boarding facilities as soon as all debts had been paid.

In requesting these assurances, Huckins indicated that he was not condemning the board for any past actions and that his suggestions were made in "love and affection." He explained that as he felt accountable to his donors so he also wanted the trustees to feel accountable for their use of the funds that he collected.[15] The trustee committee appointed to notify Huckins of his reemployment noted these stipulations and agreed to them, indicating that they would present these conditions at the next trustee meeting. They felt certain that his ideas would be agreeable to the entire board.

Huckins credited their good faith and set out once more to raise funds for the university. Until the full board could ratify the committee's personal pledges, however, Huckins's employment was not official. This the trustees did at their annual meeting on 10 June, during which they also used Huckins's requests for assurances as a catalyst to evaluate their past fiscal operations and to plan more systematically for the future. Thus Huckins, determined to ensure the proper use and management of funds that he was striving so hard to secure, indirectly initiated a master financial and development program for the university.

In June 1852, Huckins went to Marshall to attend the fifth annual session of the Baptist State Convention. He had missed the two previous conferences because of his fund-raising duties outside the state. At this convention Huckins served as a delegate from the Houston Baptist Church, the third church he had represented at various meetings of this body. In 1848, at the organization of the convention, he had represented the Independence church. The next year the Washington church had appointed him as a delegate. While his official place of residence was Independence, and he moved his membership to that church, Huckins still owned property in Galveston and maintained friendships with many people there as well as in Houston. Since the Reverend Thomas Chilton, pastor of the Houston church, was unable to attend the convention, Huckins had been requested to replace him at the meeting.

In the opening session Huckins was called upon to preach the introductory sermon in lieu of the scheduled speaker, J. B. Stiteler, who failed to attend. His sermon was based on Haggai's prophecy concerning the coming of the Messiah. Later, when he presented the report of the Education Committee, of which he was the chairman, he continued the prophetic theme, indicating that the results of a properly funded ministerial education program would "enable us to exert a vast influence upon the character and destiny of the world."[16]

Most of the preachers in Texas had necessarily come from other states, but Huckins felt that it was time for Texans to educate and train their own ministers. He was convinced that ministerial education was of "paramount importance." His educational report emphasized the role that Baylor University could play in the program.[17]

The school was continuing to grow and had just completed another term, with an enrollment of one hundred sixty-five students. The ten-thousand-dollar endowment for the presidency was almost complete, and six faculty members were currently giving "their undivided energies to the institution." In addition, two ministerial students had already completed their studies at Baylor and were "building up our Redeemer's cause in destitute and important places."[18] Huckins felt certain that, with adequate financial support, Baylor could offer a ministerial education program of high quality suitable for generations to come.

As a part of his report, he presented two resolutions. The first recommended that all churches of the state seek out from their congregations those who felt called to the ministry and then provide the funds to "enable them to make a suitable preparation for the Gospel Ministry." The second proposal encouraged all pastors to present the subject of ministerial education before their congregations at least once a year and to "adopt some plan by which regular contributions will be made to the cause of ministerial education."[19]

Huckins knew that he alone could not garner enough money for this cause, no matter how many miles he might travel and how many people he might solicit. But he felt that if pastors and congregations would work together to promote, to encourage, and to provide financial support for those who wished to become ministers, then the cause of Christ in Texas would be well served.

While the specific topic of ministerial education was the subject dearest to Huckins's heart, the general topic of Christian education seemed to attract the greatest interest at the convention. On 21 June, the third day of the meeting, when the Tyler Baptist Church recommended that the convention establish a female institute in that city, the proposition was properly submitted to a committee for review. However, when the committee reported its findings, it adopted a very narrow and strict view of the convention's role in Christian education. Subsequent analysis of the committee's stance provoked a minor, but fundamental, controversy.

Christian education had existed in Texas since the establishment of the first two Sabbath schools in 1829. There were in 1852 approximately 150 such "schools" throughout the state, and Baptists wholeheartedly endorsed these endeavors, even though most of the Sabbath schools were joint ventures of several denominations within a particular settlement or city. The denomination felt a responsibility to promote and support any program designed to encourage the study of the Bible.[20]

Many Baptists in the state also believed that the establishment and support of academies was a responsibility of the denomination, in spite of the fact that these institutions offered general education that was not specifically "religious" in character. Such schools were held to be capable of providing a proper atmosphere for learning, which could nurture students in the Christian principles upon which they might build their future lives.

In effect, this nurturing of students was what Baylor had been doing for several years, though some mistakenly believed that the institution had been established primarily for the training of preachers. Ministerial training may often have appeared to be the university's primary purpose, especially in view of the emphasis placed by Huckins and others on the importance of this type of education, but no such limitations had been expressed in its charter. Indeed, only two students had thus far been expressly preparing for the ministry while at Baylor.

In December 1851, when a proposal had been made in a Baylor trustee meeting to establish a theological department in the university, members of the board decided that the organization of such a department was inexpedient, though they did "deem it highly important that young men preparing for the ministry should have all the facilities that can be afforded them under present conditions." They therefore recommended that the president gather those interested in theology and "give them whatever instruction he may be able." They recommended that additional instruction also could be provided by the Reverend George W. Baines, pastor of the Independence Baptist Church.[21]

Thus, though theological instruction was available at Baylor, the school essentially offered a liberal arts curriculum, the same approach that the citizens of Tyler proposed for the institution in their area. The proponents of the Tyler academy even emphasized the possibility that it might become a "feeder school" for

Baylor, if students from Tyler should decide to continue their education on the university level.

The committee of the Baptist State Convention that studied the Tyler proposal for a female academy expressed approval of the "liberal educational spirit manifested" by the members of that city's Baptist church and other citizens who had conceived the idea. They even wished them "abundant success in their truly noble and praiseworthy enterprise." However, the committee felt it was

> incompatible with the constitutional province and design of the convention, to solicit and raise funds for the establishment of any literary institution; our educational efforts extending only to the aid of ministers of the Gospel; and as we have under our patronage the Baylor University designed specifically for this purpose, we cannot consistently promise aid to any other institution, nor extend to such a fostering or controlling influence.[22]

The committee therefore recommended that any female institute established in Tyler should be sponsored by the Baptist churches in that area and by the educational organizations of those associations that favored the idea. In the committee's opinion any Baptist group was free to start a school, but the convention could sponsor only education specifically related to the training of ministers. While this interpretation received official approval, it was not popular with many in the northeastern section of the state. Nor, in reality, was it in congruence with what was happening at Baylor, the convention's lone university.

FOR THE NEXT SIX MONTHS after the convention, Huckins once again engaged in his circuit-riding, fund-raising activities on behalf of Baylor. When the trustees gathered for their December session, they were met with news of Huckins's unprecedented success as well as reports of vast improvements in the internal operation of the university. The ten-thousand-dollar endowment for the presidency had been completed, existing facilities had been refurbished, additional teachers had been employed, and plans for the erection of new buildings had been formulated. Much of the success of the institution's operation was credited to the fiscal management policies instituted as a result of Huckins's terms for acceptance of his agency post for 1852.

Having attained this level of success, the trustees began to look toward opportunities for even greater achievements. One of the decisions they made to enhance the future of the institution also affected the future of James Huckins and eventually led him back into the pastoral ministry—the calling which, in his heart, he had never left. This was the resolution of the board to "raise an endowment of ten thousand dollars for the support of a professor of Physical Sciences as soon as practicable."[23] To fill this position they selected Jacob B. Stiteler, then pastor of the Galveston Baptist Church and the third minister to serve that church since Huckins had left it in January 1848.

The pastor who had succeeded Huckins was John F. Hillyer, an appointee of the Southern Baptist Convention's Board of Domestic Missions. After serving the Galveston congregation nine months, he had moved to Goliad to open a school. In March 1849, Robert H. Taliaferro assumed the pastorate of the church but left sixteen months later to become a missionary to the Choctaw Indians. Visiting ministers then preached at the church for about six months until Stiteler was installed in the pulpit on 12 January 1851.[24] Now, with the resignation of Stiteler after less than two years as their pastor, the Baptists of Galveston were once again without a minister. Recalling that Huckins had originally constituted their church and had led them in a successful drive to build their sanctuary, the congregation once more turned to him.

During the five years of his absence the church had experienced both good and bad times, but the membership had steadily increased. The congregation now comprised almost one hundred members, about half of whom were Negroes who, though they worshipped separately, were officially members of the Galveston church. There were many people in the church who had not been members when Huckins was pastor, and most were not personally acquainted with him. But almost all knew him by reputation and were convinced he was a dedicated minister of Jesus Christ.

On 5 May 1853, the congregation met and unanimously voted to request that Huckins become their pastor. A canvass of the members was then conducted to ascertain individual feelings on the matter and to determine how much each family could pay toward the pastor's salary. The canvass resulted in enthusiastic approval and four hundred dollars in guarantees.

Two weeks later the church met again and agreed upon this amount as the pastor's salary. They also voted to allow him to rent all but twenty pews, retaining the rental fees as part of his compensation. J. P. Cole, secretary of the church and a close friend of Huckins's, was instructed to notify him of the decision. By the time Cole wrote his letter, another thirty dollars had been pledged toward the proposed salary.[25]

Although anxious to return to the pastorate, Huckins was concerned whether his move to Galveston would be in the best interest of the church, himself, or the cause of Christ. He also was apprehensive about the limited salary offered. Before answering Cole's letter, he went to Huntsville to attend the annual session of the Baptist State Convention and to inquire while there about possible financial assistance from the convention's Board of Domestic Missions.[26]

The board agreed to employ Huckins as a part-time missionary at an annual salary of one hundred dollars if he should accept the call of the Galveston church. In addition, two members of the board, Baylor president Rufus C. Burleson and the Reverend Jacob Stiteler, recently resigned pastor of the Galveston congregation, agreed to write to the Southern Baptist Convention's Board of Domestic Missions to request employment for him at two hundred dollars per year.

On the final day of the convention, 23 June 1853, Huckins wrote to Cole to inform him of his inclination to become the pastor of the Galveston church, but indicated that before making a final decision he wanted the opportunity to visit the members of the church to ascertain their real feelings about his return. He felt a need to determine whether

> I can have a faithful and zealous cooperation on the part of the members in carrying [out] the great objects

for which the Church of Christ was established. Whether I am expected to be a faithful and honest pastor in the family, as well as in the pulpit, or whether I am expected merely to be the preacher and the social friend.[27]

Huckins knew he would need the prayers and confidence of the members if he were going to succeed in making the church "holy and Christ-like."

In his letter to Cole he stated that he planned to visit Galveston early in July. He suggested that the congregation make this occasion a subject of special prayer and that they take the subject into their closets with

> them, before their family altars and into the prayer meetings. For let me not go unless I go laden with the spirit of the Master. Let me not be received unless I am received by a band of praying disciples.[28]

On his way to Galveston Huckins met with the Baylor trustees at Independence. There he presented his report and a bill for his services of $803.20. This amount included a part of the salary due him for 1852 which had not been paid yet. The trustees accepted the debt and paid Huckins about half of it in cash and the remainder in the form of a draft against R. E. B. Baylor. They also requested that Huckins continue to serve as special agent for the next year, without compensation.[29]

On 10 July, Huckins arrived in Galveston. After a brief investigation, he became convinced of the seriousness of the church members and of their desire and motivation to serve Christ. By the end of the month he agreed to serve again as the pastor of the congregation.

James Huckins had traveled a long way and had been gone a long time, but he had never ceased to love the Galveston church. He was "back home" again.

11

LESS THAN A MONTH AFTER Huckins and his family settled in Galveston, yellow fever attacked the city. The dread disease had entered the United States in May through the port of New Orleans and had ravaged seacoast towns in Louisiana, Alabama, and Mississippi before slowly moving along the Texas coastline. The first cases in Galveston appeared in early August, but most people in the city felt that since the summer had been unusually cool thus far, the danger from the fever would be slight. However, the number of cases continued to mount. By 1 September 1853, the disease had reached epidemic proportions.

By no means was this the first yellow fever epidemic experienced by the people of Galveston. In 1839 25 percent of the population had died from the disease. There were also serious attacks in 1844 and 1847, but since that time illness and death from yellow fever had been infrequent.

The 1853 epidemic raged for fifteen weeks, more than twice as long as any of the previous attacks. By the time it abated, ten days before Christmas, almost 12 percent of the city's forty-five hundred residents had died.[1] Huckins spent these weeks trying to minister to those in need, not restricting his efforts just to the members of his congregation. He offered his services throughout the entire city.

> No hour night or day did he call his own; often, when completely exhausted would he throw himself on the bed for a few moments rest to be called to the bedside of the sick or dying. At one period he hardly had time to change his clothes for eleven days and nights so much was he occupied in nursing the sick and burying the dead.[2]

Huckins was heavily in demand because he was the only healthy evangelical minister in Galveston. One other had contracted the fever. Another had left the city and planned to remain away until the fever subsided.

Although Huckins was extremely busy assisting those with special needs, he tried not to neglect his own church members, leading them in prayer meetings regularly and preaching to them as often as possible. In addition, he ministered to the Negro Baptist congregation in the city and made frequent trips to the San Jacinto area to conduct worship services for a group of about fifteen Baptists living in that vicinity.

Because of these unusual conditions in Galveston, Huckins was unable to participate in the fall meeting of the Union Baptist Association. It was the first associational meeting held since his return to the pastorate. For that reason, he had hoped to attend, but the demands on him in the city were too great.

The Galveston church sent a letter to the association expressing regrets that their pastor would not be able to attend, but explained the reasons. The letter also expressed appreciation for Huckins's "ardent piety, his assiduous labor, and his faithful admonitions, but above all, his animating example" which had helped to restore the spiritual life of the members and renewed "a more devotional feeling in all our hearts."[3]

Near the end of the year, as the trauma and anxiety caused by the epidemic diminished, many citizens banded together in an attempt to form an organization to help alleviate the anguish that future outbreaks of yellow fever might thrust upon the city. During the 1844 yellow fever epidemic, several people had worked together to help the sick and dying, but no formal organization had resulted.

There were volunteer groups in many cities along the Gulf coast who served others in emergencies regardless of race, creed, or sex. Each group was autonomous and free to deal with its local problems, though some of them occasionally gave financial assistance to sister groups in other states. The first such organization of this type in the United States was established in New Orleans in 1837. Since that time almost all major seacoast cities had incorporated similar organizations. Often they took the name of the Howard Association in honor of John Howard, a late eighteenth-century British philanthropist who was noted for his attempts at social and prison reform.

Interested citizens of Galveston formed their local Howard Association on 23 March 1854. Huckins was instrumental in forming this group and became vice president some six weeks after its organization.[4]

When the seventh annual Baptist State Convention was held the third week of June, the magnitude of Huckins's labors since returning to Galveston as pastor of the Baptist church became public. In his report to the convention's Board of Domestic Missions, he indicated that he had preached 128 sermons, attended 144 prayer meetings, baptized 15 people, made more than 600 religious visits, and traveled 900 miles in pursuit of his ministerial responsibilities. He accomplished all of this in addition to his vast community service during the yellow fever epidemic and his recent participation in the Howard Association activities.[5]

Despite the taxing schedule that had strained Huckins as he tried to meet the needs of his church and community, he had not failed to promote the broader denominational missionary and educational interests. In fact, he led his church to give more money for these purposes between July 1853 and June 1854 than any other church in the Baptist State Convention.[6]

As a testimony to his special contributions and overall leadership, the delegates to this convention elected him president.[7] In this position he became an ex officio member of every convention committee, enabling him to become involved in almost all Texas Baptist activities. Because the convention voted to change the annual meeting date from June to October, Huckins's term of office would last for fifteen months instead of the usual twelve.

Huckins soon realized that the responsibility of state convention president would demand a great amount of his time and energy. One item that would demand his attention related to the possible establishment of a newspaper—a goal for which many in the denomination had been clamoring for some time. Another was the mission effort among the Indians and German population, and yet another was the need to improve support for Baylor

University. In addition, church members across the state had shown increased interest in organizing Bible societies to assist the Southern Baptist Convention's efforts to disseminate the Gospel worldwide. Finally, the establishment of more churches and preaching stations in Texas would be a growing challenge because of the rapid increase in immigration from the other states and from abroad. As president of the convention, Huckins committed himself to try to achieve progress in all these areas.

Added to all these responsibilities was yet another which faced him upon his return to Galveston in July. Yellow fever had again struck the city. As an officer of the Howard Association, Huckins was called upon for the next several weeks to attend weekly meetings, to contact physicians to secure their assistance, to participate in a fund-raising drive, and to handle numerous administrative assignments. During this time he was requested again and again to minister to the sick and dying. There were practically no nurses available, and the few physicians in the city were impossibly overburdened. Traversing Galveston by day and by night, Huckins attempted to console the hundreds of bereaved and to assist the sick in any way possible. His own wife and his cook were soon added to the list of those stricken with the fever, thus adding personal grief to the burden of concern he carried for the entire city.

As winter approached, the death total continued to mount. Although those in Huckins's house recovered, more than four hundred others in the city did not. The Howard Association played a major role in funding funeral costs for many of these people, as well as providing vast quantities of supplies and medical services to others.

By the end of 1854, Galveston returned to normal. The scars of the epidemic were short-lived, except upon the emotions of those who had suffered, and there were many in this category. A large majority of them had been touched by the ministry of James Huckins.

12

HUCKINS BEGAN 1855 with a renewed desire to devote more attention to his church and to his denominational responsibilities. The next few months presented unusual opportunities for him to do so.

In late March, Wesley Smith, a Methodist minister, published a treatise on baptism in the pages of the *Texas Christian Advocate*, the state's Methodist newspaper. Smith's thesis that sprinkling was the correct means of administering baptism so angered Huckins that he felt it his duty as a Baptist minister, and particularly as the elected leader of the Baptist denomination in Texas, to reply to Smith's article in an effort to point out the pertinent errors of his interpretation of the Scriptures. This he did in April through the pages of *The Texas Baptist*. This newspaper had begun publication in January under the editorship of George W. Baines and was considered the "official" Baptist voice in Texas.

Huckins's article brought a swift rebuke from Smith in a subsequent issue of the *Advocate*, which in turn was answered by Huckins in *The Texas Baptist*. Citing specific definitions of Greek words and phrases, Huckins gave examples of historical interpretations and practices. Smith refuted these again, and the debate continued in ensuing issues of each paper, often becoming more personal than doctrinal on Smith's part.[1]

As Huckins attempted to defend the fundamental Baptist practice of baptism by immersion, he began to experience within his church an unusual spirit of fellowship and interest in the Bible. Capacity crowds so filled the prayer meetings that participants had "hardly enough room to kneel and after a while scarce enough breath to sing."[2] The worship services also were well attended, with visitors from the Presbyterian and Methodist churches often in the audience. Any attempt to correlate directly the spiritual renewal of many of the Galveston Baptist Church members with the publicity generated by Huckins's defense of the Baptist position on baptism would rest upon mere speculation. It is evident, however, that the congregation did grow closer spiritually during the several weeks of debates between Huckins and Smith.

Because of the support he was receiving from his church members during this time, Huckins embarked upon yet another crusade—the "discontinuance of all worldly occupations on the Sabbath" in Galveston. Working with city aldermen, other ministers, and interested citizens, his influence gradually began to be felt. In late spring, regulations restricting the types of businesses that could operate on Sundays were approved.[3] It was a clear victory for Huckins's efforts.

The success that Huckins was experiencing in his ministry inspired many in his church. It took the city's Presbyterians and Methodists, however, to spark this flame of inspiration and give the Baptist congregation a burning desire to put their faith into action. That action manifested itself in refurbishment of the church building as a physical witness to their renewed faith.

The cosmopolitan character and social sophistication of the people of Galveston in the mid-1850s gave an advantage to church groups that employed a more formal style of worship. The most successful in the city were the Catholics and Episcopalians, both of whom practiced liturgical services. The evangelical churches, which tended to employ more "emotional extemporization," usually attracted smaller crowds.[4] Among the latter group were the Baptists, Methodists, and Presbyterians.

Because of the perennial desire for more members, a sense of competition existed among these churches. Any advance by one of them in attracting prospective members necessitated a similar response from the others. Since the Baptist meeting house had been dedicated in September 1847, little had been done to make it more attractive and inviting. In May, when the Presbyterians and Methodists started renovating their worship centers, the Baptists were compelled to follow their examples. They immediately started a campaign to raise funds for the refurbishment of their sanctuary. By the end of the month they had collected a sufficient amount to whitewash and paint the interior and to recarpet the aisles and pulpit area.[5]

The enthusiasm generated within the congregation by the redecoration of the meeting house, coupled with the spiritual renewal that had taken place earlier in the year, seemed to ensure a promising future of growth. However, during the summer of 1855, the church experienced a setback. Unusually rainy weather frequently prohibited the Sunday school and worship services, and the island's excessive heat as well as a gnawing fear of the return of yellow fever drove many members away from the city. With this exodus the church programs were all but forgotten. Not until fall, when the cooler weather ended the threat of yellow fever, did the church begin to return to normal. By that time, however, much of the eagerness and excitement prevalent in the spring had diminished.

On 5 October 1855, the Union Baptist Association met in Brenham for their sixteenth annual session. It was the first associational meeting that Huckins had been able to attend since his return to the Galveston church, and the delegates gave clear evidence that they were glad he was there. On Friday he delivered the introductory sermon; on Saturday he addressed the Texas Baptist Education Society; on Sunday he preached at the Methodist Episcopal church; and on Monday he was appointed to the Printing Committee.[6]

During the meeting he also was named to a special committee. Along with Rufus Burleson and J. W. D. Creath, he was to "visit the First Baptist Church in Houston, and endeavor, by preaching and by prayer, to resuscitate the same, and induce them to be represented in this body as heretofore."[7]

The Houston church had experienced difficulty in maintaining its vitality since Burleson's departure in 1851 to assume the presidency of Baylor University. He had been followed by Thomas H. Chilton, whose ministry had brought many new members into the church. Unfortunately, when Chilton left in 1853, the congregation split. No regular services had been held there for more than two years.

Huckins accepted the task of reviving the second church he

had constituted in Texas with some reluctance because of the almost overwhelming burden of responsibilities under which he was already laboring. The magnitude of the tasks before him and the "thought of the great responsibility of his calling" often led him to the brink of despair. Only the support of his friends in Galveston and across the country encouraged him to press onward. He knew that "he could not give up, that he must succeed at last."[8]

Three weeks later, when the Baptist State Convention met at Independence, Huckins's dedication to his religious calling and his indefatigable spirit became known. Since taking office as president of the convention in June 1854, he had ministered to a city under a yellow-fever shroud of death, had repeatedly defended publicly the Baptist position on baptism, and had led his church in mounting a campaign of refurbishment that had carried over into its mission gifts, which again were the largest among all the churches in the convention. In addition, he had preached 104 sermons, delivered 52 exhortations and other addresses, traveled to numerous cities on missionary visits, and constantly ministered to both the white and black congregations in Galveston.[9]

During the fifteen months of his presidency, the convention had witnessed an unusual prosperity. A newspaper had been started, previously established mission stations had grown, and new mission endeavors among the Indians and Germans had begun. In addition, the enrollment at Baylor had continued to climb, and fund-raising drives for new facilities at the institution had been most successful. Delegates to the convention were greatly pleased by the progress of their denomination and, recognizing the importance of Huckins's leadership in these achievements, they reelected him as president for another year.[10]

13

IN 1856 AS TEXAS STOOD ready to enter its second decade as a component member of the United States of America, most of the major adjustments from republic to state had been completed. Political and economic problems still existed, Indian conflicts still occurred, and the criminal element was still present. A revival of progress was occurring, however, as cities grew, transportation improved, and financial conditions stabilized.

The Baptists in the state also were experiencing a revival of progress with "increased spirituality and Christian charity," and an unusual fervor to share the love of Christ was manifested in many of their endeavors.[1] A spirit of harmony enlivened the denomination as evidenced through increased giving. James Huckins, who gave 25 percent of his income from the Texas Baptist Board of Domestic Missions back to the convention for missionary purposes and contributed generously to the various educational causes, exemplified the generous spirit of Texas Baptists.

During the first half of the year, Huckins spent much of his time promoting denominational endeavors and guiding the spiritual development of the Galveston and Houston congregations. He averaged almost four visits a week to the homes of those to whom he ministered and attended at least six prayer meetings each month, besides preaching twice nearly every Sunday. The weight of his responsibilities only added zeal to his drive to accomplish all he could for Christ.

Summer again brought on fear of yellow fever in Galveston. The Howard Association, with Huckins as a vital component, increased its activities in preparation for an onslaught of the disease. The fears proved groundless, however, as the fever never reached the Texas coast, perhaps because of unusually dry weather that lasted until early fall.

In October, Huckins participated in the Union Baptist Association meeting in Coldspring. Discussions at this gathering focused upon developments at Baylor University and upon the status of *The Texas Baptist*.

Baylor's future seemed assured. The male department had about 150 students and the females numbered close to 100. A three-story building for the women was nearing completion, and plans were being made to enlarge the overcrowded facilities occupied by the men. There was still an indebtedness of some eleven hundred dollars on the improvements currently underway on the campus, but the trustees were confident that the funds could be raised relatively soon.[2]

The university's report to the association, prepared by trustee chairman Hosea Garrett, indicated

> The Professors and Teachers continue to command the public confidence in a very high degree, while a healthy tone or moral feeling has pervaded the entire institution. The most cordial relations exist between the Trustees and teachers, also between the latter and students.[3]

Everything at Baylor appeared harmonious, prosperous, and promising. Indeed it was, at least to the public eye. However, there was a controversy brewing between the president of the university and the head of its female department that would eventually create a serious disruption to the educational activities of the institution.

Horace Clark, having been employed as principal of the female department, felt that complete responsibility for this department was his—that he was answerable only to the trustees. Rufus Burleson, as president of the university, believed that he should have responsibility for the administrative operations of the entire institution, which included the female department. Although the trustees were aware of the controversy, thus far they had taken no official actions to solve it because it had not yet caused any major hindrances to the operation of the institution.

In addition to this problem, another one was arising on the Texas Baptist educational horizon. It had started four years before when the Baptist State Convention had voted not to establish an educational institution in Tyler. Many Baptists in the eastern part of Texas felt this rejection had been motivated by sectionalism, so within a short time they created their own convention and their own university. Although the members of the "eastern" convention publicly proclaimed a desire to cooperate with their brethren in the "western" convention, this cooperation was primarily in matters of faith and principles. Behind the appeal for unity, there was a spirit of educational competitiveness that later would detract from the hope of many for Baylor to become the one and only university for all Baptists in the state.

These educational developments were of some concern to the delegates at the October associational meeting in Coldspring, but the status of the denominational paper—*The Texas Baptist*—generated much more interest. Communication of religious information had been a matter of importance to Baptists in Texas for nearly two decades. Shortly after the establishment of the Union Association in 1840, the *Baptist Banner and Western Pioneer* held the status of "official" voice of Texas Baptists. It gave way to the *South Western Baptist Chronicle* when that organ began operation in New Orleans in the mid-1850s. Of course other Baptist periodicals were read by Texas Baptists—especially those printed in Georgia, Tennessee, and Alabama—but the distinctiveness of Texas spirit practically demanded its own native paper.

Committees had been authorized by the Baptist State Convention in 1852 and 1853 to investigate the feasibility of establishing a Baptist paper with headquarters at Independence. Supporters were unable to raise sufficient funds to initiate the paper in that town, but in 1854 several individuals agreed to assume financial responsibility for its first year of operation if its publication offices could be located in Anderson.

In January 1855 after several years of discussion and planning, George W. Baines and J. B. Stiteler, as editor and assistant editor respectively, produced the first issue of *The Texas Baptist*. During the year more than one thousand subscriptions were recorded, but these did not provide enough income to fund the operation. At the June 1855 Baptist State Convention, recommendations for the assumption of its financial liability by the convention had failed, causing the editors to resort to private sources in order to continue publication for another year.

The Texas Baptist had been generally accepted as the "official voice" of all Baptists in the state, and most seemed pleased with Baines's efforts. However, the perpetual state of crisis engendered by operating on an annual basis presented very real obstacles to the effectiveness of the publication. If the future of the newspaper was to be assured, the number of subscriptions would have to be increased greatly. Realizing this, representatives at the Union Association meeting passed several resolutions calling for all Texas Baptists "to identify ourselves with its interests" and to "make it a matter of individual concern to increase the circulation of the paper." The resolutions also requested that all subscriptions be paid in cash in order to facilitate the purchase of new type and equipment.[4]

Later in October when Huckins presided at the Baptist State Convention, it was evident the concerns relating to education and the newspaper were on the minds of Baptists around the state and not just those in the Union Association. At this meeting in Anderson the delegates affirmed their support for Baylor and *The Texas Baptist* with reports and resolutions calling for increased giving to the university and for placing the newspaper on a "more sure and settled basis." In addition to these matters, the convention passed proposals designed to aid the distribution of religious books, to encourage the formation of temperance societies, and "to elevate the standard of Sabbath School instruction."[5]

The prevailing atmosphere during the convention was one of "general unanimity of sentiment and harmony of feeling." As the assembly adjourned, those who had participated returned to their homes and areas of responsibility reassured that there had "been a much greater amount of time, labor, and money devoted to the causes of our holy religion during the last year, within our bounds, than in any two years past."[6] Huckins was pleased that his work as president of the Baptist State Convention during the past twelve months had been a pleasant and successful one. Since he had been reelected to another term, he looked forward to the challenges and opportunities the coming year would bring him and his fellow laborers for Christ.

14

SOON AFTER RETURNING TO GALVESTON from the state convention, Huckins began to notice subtle changes in the prayer meetings of his church. The men and women still gathered separately for devotions and prayer. But while the women's sessions were filled with emotion as in the past, the tenor of the men's groups was different. Whereas Huckins and one or two other men had formerly been the only persons who talked and prayed, now, little by little, others began to express themselves openly until gradually all the men were participating verbally.

This involvement by so many men was such a surprise and delight to Huckins that he wrote about it in a report to the Southern Baptist Board of Domestic Missions. When the board's monthly publication carried news of this development, the information was picked up and published in other Baptist periodicals, often with comments by the editors.

The editor of the *South Western Baptist* in Alabama congratulated Huckins for "having the oversight [sic] of such a church" and emphasized the uniqueness of the situation. He compared the Galveston men to the old Puritans who were not afraid to speak out and derided the taciturn masculine attitudes that prevailed in many Baptist churches. He wrote,

> Many of them are so polite and unobtrusive that many conclude their 'room is good company' at prayer meetings, and do not attend; and, they carry their politeness so far in another respect, that they allow preachers to do all the public speaking in the Church.[1]

The editor concluded his comments with a promise that "Should it ever occur in the providence of God that we should pass through Galveston, we will call to see that *strange* church, that *peculiar* people."[2]

Huckins was thankful not only for evidences of renewed spirituality in his members, but also for the results of their prayers that were being manifested in the almost monthly baptismal services. Even though the church rolls fluctuated because of population shifts as people moved in and out of the city, active membership averaged around ninety.

During the early months of 1857, Huckins began to limit his travels around the state in order to devote more time to community affairs, especially to the Howard Association. Although there was no yellow fever present in Galveston during this time, the association, nevertheless, remained active and continued to make plans to meet any future needs that might be brought on by the disease.

One of the association's special activities during the spring was a fund-raising campaign. Due to Huckins's broad experience in this kind of work and because of the esteem with which he was held by so many of the citizens of Galveston, he was selected to be one of the leaders of this drive. In spite of this time-consuming special concern, the matter of ministerial education remained uppermost in Huckins's thoughts. He continually sought ways to encourage contributions to this cause. It was Huckins's desire

> that the Baptist denomination in Texas shall, ere long, present to the world not only an efficient and learned ministry, but give a wise ministry of marked intelligency, thoroughly educated in whatever is useful and good, and especially in the science of human redemption.[3]

WHEN THE BAPTIST STATE CONVENTION met in October 1857, Huckins led the opening prayer and delivered the keynote address, concluding his presidency of almost three and a quarter years, the longest continuous service in this position since the Convention had been founded in 1848. However, his service to the convention was not over yet. Through the years

Huckins had constantly advocated the development of programs of assistance for students who were preparing for the ministry in institutions of higher education, especially at Baylor. Because of his deep interest in this matter, the convention delegates elected him chairman of a special committee on ministerial education.

In August 1857, Huckins had been elected a vice president of the Southern Baptist Bible Board, the arm of the convention responsible for the dissemination of Bibles and religious literature. When he gave the report of the special committee on ministerial education on the floor of the Baptist State Convention, it was evident that his lifelong concern for better ministerial education, his extensive travels across the country witnessing the needs and various approaches to meet them, and his recent involvement with the Bible Board all had combined to nurture the novel recommendation that the committee suggested. The resolution that he proposed invited the convention to consider the "propriety of extending aid in books to such men as seem to possess the requisite gifts of the Christian ministry, and who are unable to pursue a course of collegiate study."[4] Though not revolutionary, it was, nevertheless, an innovative idea for Texas Baptists to evaluate.

There were only three young men at Baylor then preparing for the ministry, yet there was "a great number of destitute churches . . . entirely deprived of the gospel of Jesus, and which are sending up one prolonged cry, 'Send us a Baptist minister.'"[5] Huckins had heard this call many times over the past three years while serving as convention president. To meet this need he wanted to join the available printed resources with the available human resources.

The committee's report asked,

> Are there not men even now amongst us, already called of God to preach the Gospel, but who are unlearned, and yet who are too far advanced in life, and too heavily burdened with the cases of life to receive an education at the schools, and yet who have such gifts and graces, and such strong common sense, that they would be eminently useful in leading sinners to Christ?[6]

An affirmative response was implicit, because the report then indicated that these middle-aged men could "educate themselves and become mighty in the Scriptures" if only they could be given "suitable books and suitable management."[7] Huckins wanted the convention to develop a program to procure appropriate printed matter and to provide it to those who were called to the ministry, but who were forced by circumstances to follow the path of self-education. This was evident in the conclusion of the report which inquired,

> Would not this course be the means of furnishing our famishing churches with the bread of life, and supplying those lost fields of destitution on our coast and frontier with just such missionaries as are needed by the people, and as God would bless?[8]

The convention agreed with Huckins and his committee and voted to study the proposal to determine its potential for building up churches all over the state.

When the convention closed, the delegates' spirits were high, their motivation intense. A new opportunity for the spread of the Gospel was in their grasp. Huckins had served well as president, leading the denomination to a new plateau of prosperity and leaving office with a challenge that might raise its prosperity ever higher in the future. It was a giant step toward elevating the level of Baptist religious education in Texas.

HUCKINS HAD BEEN INVOLVED in denominational activities for several years, but now he planned to concentrate only upon his preferred form of service—the pastoral ministry. He declined continued employment with both the Texas and Southern Baptist mission boards because he wanted to spend more time ministering to his congregation and not be required by such employment to travel to mission points around the state. He also was more financially secure now and did not feel the necessity of relying upon funding from these boards.

The source of his improved financial condition had come through business dealings, primarily the sale and trade of town lots, since his return to Galveston in 1853, but he also had made some profits in another endeavor. Since purchasing his first slave for household chores, he had bought and sold other bondsmen. Through this means he had been able to accumulate some money, though the actual amount is not known.[9]

Huckins had only a few months to concentrate his labors within the Galveston church before his election to the presidency of the Howard Association in May 1858 demanded a broader community involvement. The Howard Association had held only quarterly meetings since late 1856, when the menace of yellow fever had faded. Now with the dread disease already rampant in the eastern United States, citizens of Galveston were becoming concerned. In order to ensure optimum operational readiness for the possible arrival of the fever, Huckins called for more frequent sessions of the association and instituted programs to solicit contributions.

Later, when numerous cases of yellow fever were reported in the city, Huckins was compelled to organize new fund-raising endeavors. These were so successful that by the middle of September the association was able to distribute hundreds of dollars for food, shelter, medical, and even burial expenses to those requiring these services. Several children whose parents died even received free transportation to relatives in other states.

Huckins was extremely involved in all the Howard Association activities, but because of his ministerial vocation, his responsibilities to the citizens of Galveston did not end with humanitarian relief programs; he also had to serve as an ambassador of Christ. Remembering his devoted assistance during the epidemics of 1853 and 1854, people throughout the city called on him again and again to come to their aid. As in the past, he responded freely, day and night.

It was late November before the epidemic abated. During the weeks it had gripped Galveston, Huckins had dedicated so much of his time to the community's needs that he had not been able to direct the affairs of his church as he would have preferred; nor had he been able to attend any denominational meetings. He had preached when he could to both the black and white congregations, but the requirements of the sick and dying had demanded that his pastoral role for the city take precedence over the work of his church. In December 1858, in an effort to moderate the continuing pressures upon Huckins and in order to have more regular services as well, both the white and black congregations of the Galveston Baptist Church requested assistance from other sources.

The white members invited the Reverend J. H. Stribling to come to Galveston to "spend some weeks laboring with us and for our good." Stribling, the first ministerial student ever enrolled at Baylor University, had been baptized by William Tryon in 1843 and had been ordained in 1849. He had served several churches in the Colorado River valley and was well known across the state.[10]

The black congregation, a branch of the Galveston church though they met in their own building, had always shared a minister with the white members. Now, because of their desire "that the ordinances of the church be administered by their pastor at their own house of worship," they issued a call to the Reverend James Langley to become their pastor. The white members were required to sanction this action, and they readily did so.[11] After both ministers agreed to come to Galveston, the white and black congregations happily anticipated the new year.

The sacrifices that Huckins had made in ministering to the community were well-recognized and appreciated by the majority of the citizens in Galveston, but some people in his own church were less generously disposed. Prominent among the latter was George Fellows, a charter member who had been active in the church's building program in 1847. He had disliked Huckins since 1844, when he had passed by his pastor's house one day and heard sounds that indicated Huckins was beating his household slave. On several occasions Fellows had expressed his displeasure with Huckins to others, both in and out of the church.[12] Though he continued to work with his pastor, he was not a loyal supporter. Particularly during the late fall of 1858 when the yellow fever epidemic diverted so much of Huckins's time from his church duties, Fellows had attempted to undermine his ministry.

In a business meeting in early January 1859, he proposed that the church inform Huckins that "we cannot consider it his duty to longer waste his time, talents, and energies upon it [the church]." While it was true that Huckins's preaching had not been regular because of the enormous demands upon his time by so many other matters, the majority of the members of the church recognized that he had not neglected his calling as a servant of Christ and voted to table Fellows's motion.[13] In February, Stribling arrived at Galveston to assist Huckins and the church with such ministerial duties as might be required. This "team" approach was satisfactory for the moment and allowed Huckins more time to administer the operations of the Howard Association as it continued to meet—though less frequently—into the winter and early spring.

In May 1859, Huckins was reelected president of the Howard Association and also a vice president of the Southern Baptist Bible Board. Two years earlier, when Huckins first had been elected to the board, his involvement had given him new insights into alternatives for ministerial education and had brought about a change in thinking on this subject among Texas Baptists. This time, Huckins's involvement would indirectly lead to another change—a change that would bring about his relocation to another state and involve him personally in a devastating war.

15

ON 21 JUNE 1859, HUCKINS and his wife left Galveston by ship to visit friends in the eastern states. There were several Baptist denominational meetings scheduled that summer and early fall. Presumably Huckins attended some of them, particularly the Bible Board meetings in Nashville.

After participating in various denominational conferences, Huckins began his sea voyage back to Texas, stopping along the way to visit friends and preach. When he and his wife arrived in Charleston, South Carolina, during the third week in October, he was requested to speak to the congregation of the Wentworth Street Baptist Church who were suffering from the recent resignation of their pastor, the Reverend Basil Manly.

Manly had come to the church in 1855 after spending seventeen years as president of the University of Alabama. He was widely known and respected throughout the Southern Baptist Convention. It had been to Manly, serving a short time as president of the convention's Board of Domestic Missions, that Gail Borden, on behalf of the Galveston church, had written in March 1846 seeking news of Huckins who was then in the South raising money for the church's building program.

Manly had attempted to resign from the Wentworth Street church at the end of 1858. However, because of the congregation's pleas for him to reconsider, he relented and stayed six more months.[1] Since his departure in June, the church had invited various ministers to conduct worship services. Frequently, when no preachers were available, services had not been held.

Established in November 1840 as an outgrowth of the First Baptist Church, the Wentworth Street Baptist Church had more than four hundred members. In addition to its original building, erected in 1842 as a worship center, it also owned a three-year-old lecture and Sunday school building, where thirteen teachers instructed about seventy people in weekly scriptural lessons. The library of the church contained more than eight hundred volumes.[2]

The announcement that Huckins would preach at the church was carried in the *Charleston Daily Courier* of Saturday, 29 October 1859. Large crowds assembled the next day at both morning and evening sessions to hear him. Because of the impression he made, he was requested to return the following two Sundays, after which the church asked him to become the pastor.[3]

When Huckins returned to Galveston the first week of December, he immediately wrote a letter of resignation to the Galveston Baptist Church. He had served that congregation for almost fourteen years during his two terms as pastor. As the first church he had constituted in Texas, it was still the church of his heart.

The decision to leave Galveston was a difficult one for Huckins as he had thought he would remain there for the rest of his life. "But God orders it differently," he wrote in his letter to the church. "His will manifestly is that you and I should separate, that you should seek another pastor, and that I should enter another field. I submit to that will, tho it slay me—tho it crush all my dearest hopes."[4]

Emphasizing his undying love for the church, he stated,

> Brethren you shall live in my heart and in my prayers. Your prosperity shall be my joy; your adversity my grief. I pray that you may have better pastors in years to come, than I have been, holier men and vastly more efficient. But, brethren, No pastor will ever love you as I have done.[5]

When his resignation was presented to the church following the Sunday morning service on 11 December, the congregation accepted it with an effective date of 1 January 1860. J. P. Cole and P. S. Bargiza were instructed to respond in the name of the church with a return letter to Huckins. Their communication, written the next day, was one of love and appreciation for the years of dedicated service that Huckins had given to the church and to the Galveston community. They indicated their sorrow that the "weak and depressed condition" of the church should have prompted Huckins's decision to leave and expressed the hope that "the painful separation" might serve as a lesson to church members and arouse them from their lethargy.

Regarding Huckins's unique devotion to the citizens of Galveston, they wrote,

> the universal expression, in view of your departure, has been that we may indeed fill our pulpit, but who is to take your place at the bedside of the sick and dying? Who comfort the afflicted widow? Who attend to the wants of the destitute Orphan? From many a desolate hearth, a cry of remonstrance and regret reaches our ears; and from an hundred humble dwellings of the poor, the prayers of those, whom you have comforted and relieved, mingle with ours to the Great Father of all, that, wherever you may go, and wherever labor, the work of the Lord may prosper in your hands, and that you may long live to see and enjoy the fruit of your labors of love.[6]

The letter was read before the entire church on Sunday, 18 December, and then sent to Huckins.

During the next week a minor but symbolic coincidence completed the cycle of Huckins's ministry in Texas. Mirabeau B. Lamar, former president of the Republic of Texas, died on 19 December and was to be buried in the Masonic Cemetery in Richmond, where Huckins had journeyed often to minister to the Baptists in that area. As a Mason, and as a well-known minister, and perhaps because he had been a friend of Lamar's, Huckins was asked to assist in the services of interment.[7]

Some twenty years earlier, Huckins's first official introduction to Texas had been in the form of a letter written for him by James Boykin of Columbus, Georgia, on 7 January 1840. The letter, addressed to Lamar who was then president of the country, explained Huckins's purpose in going to Texas to "arrange for the preaching of the Gospel of Christ to those over whom our creator has called you to govern."[8] Boykin had known Lamar in Columbus in the early 1830s, and had become friends with Huckins when he was in Georgia as an agent with the American Baptist Home Mission Society in 1839. When Huckins led the final prayer at Lamar's funeral, he simultaneously marked the close of the statesman's life and his own career as a servant of Christ in Texas.

On the last day of the year, Huckins's devotion to the people of Galveston was recognized by many of the leading citizens in an open letter of affection and gratitude. In it they acknowledged his "benevolent operations in the city for years past" and the way he "had often persevered in his labor of love when prudent regard to his own life would have dictated repose and quiet."[9] A few days later, on 9 January 1860, the Howard Association also publicly acknowledged his contributions to the city in glowing words of tribute, thanking him for his "efficient service as a member and President" and expressing "their admiration of the pure philanthropy and active beneficence which were conspicuous in his life and character."[10]

JAMES HUCKINS PREACHED his first sermon as pastor of Wentworth Street Baptist Church on Sunday, 23 January 1860. It was his seventh pastorate, and this congregation of about four hundred almost equalled the total membership of all of his previous churches.

For this special service the words to an old hymn were rearranged by one of the members to befit the occasion. In Huckins's honor the congregation stood and sang,

> Lord! thy presence now attend,
> Him we to Thy care commend,
> Nor a pilgrim let him rove
> Without conduct of Thy grace.
> Fire his love—enlarge his heart—
> Zeal and utterance impart.

Make him strong—his aim make pure.
Free salvation be his theme.

Then while many throng around,
From his lips to hear the sound,
Lord! vouchsafe the word to bless,
Crown his labors with success.
Guard him by Thy mighty power
Till life's work of love is o'er;
Then a crown immortal give,
Deck'd with jewels he has won.[11]

Though this was his inaugural service, formal recognition of his assumption of the pastorate did not take place until 29 February. At that time the members of all the churches in the city were invited to attend and be witnesses to the charge brought by the pastor of the First Baptist Church. In a brief but meaningful ceremony, the people officially welcomed Huckins to his place of responsibility in Charleston.[12]

While Huckins made a new home in Charleston, his family remained in Galveston to settle financial affairs. On leaving Galveston, Huckins had owned eight town lots for which no arrangements for sale had been made prior to his departure. In April his wife, Rhoda, sold the lots to Allen Lewis for nine thousand dollars. Payment was in the form of three promissory notes, the first of which was due 1 January 1861. The other two were to be paid on the first day of January of each of the following two years.[13] After the sale, Rhoda Huckins and her daughters Sarah, then twenty years old, and Mary, six years younger, journeyed to Charleston to join Huckins. Their oldest daughter, Caroline, born in Massachusetts in 1833, remained in Galveston.

WHILE RHODA HUCKINS WAS IN Texas making arrangements to begin a new and different life in South Carolina, circumstances in that eastern seaboard state were developing that would soon bring a new and different life to all Americans. During the last week of April 1860, the Democratic Party held its national convention in Charleston to select a presidential candidate. Bickering between northern and southern delegates split the convention, and after fifty-seven fruitless ballots the Democrats adjourned. When they reconvened in Baltimore in June, the Northern faction refused to seat the southern delegates, who then assembled a rump session across town and nominated John Breckinridge as their candidate. Meanwhile the northern Democrats nominated Stephen Douglas to bear the party's standard. Political fever ran high during the early weeks of summer, and many in the South, especially in Charleston, vowed secession if Abraham Lincoln, who had been selected by the Republicans, should be elected.

During this same period, some of Huckins's friends in Galveston, in a spontaneous act designed to demonstrate their continuing affection and their remembrance "with gratitude" of his "untiring devotion to the sick and destitute" in the city, contributed more than seven hundred dollars to purchase a gift for him. Approximately two hundred dollars of this money was used to commission a New York artisan to make a "massive silver pitcher and a pair of goblets." These were sent to Huckins in July along with the remaining five hundred dollars.[14]

This gift of love was reported in several Baptist newspapers, one of which was the *South Western Baptist* of Alabama, which printed that the money had been raised by members of the Galveston church and other citizens of the city. Huckins, though appreciative of the gifts and the public recognition given to the affection which the gifts represented, felt a need to take issue with this report. In a letter to the editor of the newspaper Huckins pointed out his "slight error" and indicated that the church had "nothing to do with the donations" even though "some of them would have done so most cordially, but were not permitted." He explained that the gesture was "carried through by the citizens, and was designed by them as a token of their affection for me. No Baptist, directly or indirectly, had anything to do with the affair."[15]

He requested that his letter be published, "to give the honor solely where it belongs," and concluded it by saying,

The Baptists in Galveston are doing nobly for their new pastor, and are a liberal band of brethren. They have my heart and prayers. They are my children in Christ and I can never cease to love them.[16]

As he had been in Texas, Huckins attempted to be part of as many denominational activities as possible. During the last week of July, he represented the Wentworth Street church as well as the Charleston Association at the fortieth anniversary of the State Convention of South Carolina. The main thrust of the convention activities, held at Greenville, related to the promotion of Sunday schools. Of the seven churches in the Charleston Association, the Wentworth Street church was one of only three operating a Sunday school. The others, First Baptist and Citadel Square, had programs of about the same size as that at Huckins's church.[17]

AS HUCKINS BECAME WELL KNOWN in Charleston, his reputation as an elocutionist spread across the state, affording him many opportunities to speak before various groups. As a vice president of the Southern Baptist Bible Board, Huckins had become acquainted with members of the Southern Baptist Publication Society. When the society held its annual meeting during the last week of August, Huckins was selected as the featured speaker.

His speech presented almost a portrait in miniature of the things for which he had labored during his life. It stressed the value of education, the need to publish and disseminate more religious material, the importance of developing a supply of local talent to meet local needs rather than depending upon external support, and the enjoyment of giving, both to the giver and to the receiver.

Huckins decried the long-established tradition in the publishing field whereby most of the religious material was written and published in the North and abroad. Such publications often were not fit to read, Huckins told the members and guests of the society, because they were filled with interpretations favoring the antislavery view. He displayed one such book, which was intended as a prize book for Sunday school children and said it "was found to be as full of the spirit of abolition as a pig is of meat." He believed that books to be read by Southerners should be written by Southerners and advocated that more people in the South should begin to write religious material.[18]

He told his audience that since May 1860 he had read seven manuscripts submitted to him for review prior to acceptance for publication by the society. All had been written by men from the South, and Huckins hoped that this represented a trend. He then encouraged the Baptists of the South to develop ways "to publish, to pay the authors, and to put the books in circulation." He announced his desire that "this demand for Southern-made books may be increased a thousand fold."[19]

Huckins was of the opinion that only those who knew and understood the South could adequately write for the South. He concluded his address by challenging the society to give "the sons and daughters of the South, the true interpretation of the word of God, the doctrines and ordinances of Jesus, in the primitive purity and simplicity."[20]

The sentiments regarding Northern influence and overt acts of aggression against the Southern way of life as expressed by Huckins were shared not only by those in his audience, but also by most of his constituents, his colleagues, and indeed the majority of the people of the South. For many years gaps had been developing between Northern and Southern attitudes in several areas. The strains and pressures of the coming presidential election were serving to widen the fissures.

On 6 November 1860, Lincoln won the largest vote of any of the four candidates. He was declared the president-elect of the United States even though he had failed to obtain an absolute majority. Almost immediately the South Carolina legislature voted to call a secession convention to consider alternatives for future action.

When the 109th session of the Charleston Baptist Association was held on 17 November, the proceedings were overshadowed by an atmosphere of apprehension. At this meeting Huckins represented the Wentworth Street church, the Southern Baptist Publication Society, and the Charleston-based newspaper, *The Southern Baptist*, whose agency he had recently accepted.

The report of the Wentworth Street church indicated that since Huckins's arrival in January the church had experienced a growth of more than 50 members, 5 of them by baptism. The Sunday school enrollment had not increased, but 50 volumes had been added to the church's library. Of the 477 members, 167 were Negroes.[21]

The following month the Secession Convention met in Charleston, having moved from Columbia, their original meeting place, because of a smallpox scare. The convention quickly adopted an Ordinance of Secession that declared South Carolina an independent republic. When this news reached the citizens on the streets, it was met by the "pealing of church bells mingled with the roar of saluting guns."[22]

Over the next few days, enthusiasm increased as militia companies began to assemble. Though South Carolina had had a state militia since 1841, most of the units were little more than social clubs that held quarterly meetings to practice drilling. A few companies had sensed trouble brewing in mid-1860 and had begun to meet more frequently. Some new units had even formed during the presidential campaign, but the South Carolina militia was more a paper force than a real fighting force.

ON THE EVENING OF 26 DECEMBER, United States troops stationed on Fort Moultrie, at the northern entrance of the main shipping channel to Charleston, disabled the guns of the fort and quietly moved across the channel to the more easily defensible Fort Sumter. When their actions were discovered the next day, South Carolina troops retaliated by capturing Castle Pinckney, a small fortification at the mouth of the Cooper River across the channel from the city of Charleston. The handful of federal soldiers at this site offered no resistance to the South Carolinians, who then occupied Fort Moultrie and began to repair the damages and to fortify the facility.

By early January 1861, Charleston

> seemed transformed into a military camp, companies from the upper countries came hurrying to the seacoast, batteries were being erected at all points. There

was constant drilling and nightly patrolling of the streets.[23]

On 9 January, the steamer *Star of the West*, crowded with troops to reinforce the soldiers at Fort Sumter, was turned away by South Carolina cannons. This small victory reinforced the belief held by the people of Charleston that Southern soldiers could win any war that might occur. This feeling of superiority was intensified during the next few weeks as the citizens watched the construction of an ironclad floating battery, somewhat resembling a two-story barn with four doors in the upper portion. This "ship" was to be floated near Fort Sumter so that cannons could fire through its four doorways at the stronghold's defenses.

Crowds assembled at the wharf nearest Fort Sumter on 15 March to celebrate the completion of the "transport," which was then floated to the west end of Sullivan's Island near Fort Moultrie. On 12 April, in conjunction with other South Carolina batteries, soldiers from the "barn" began to shell Fort Sumter. The roars of the cannons beckoned the citizenry of Charleston, who gathered upon the rooftops and lined the harbor seeking vantage points from which to watch the United States and South Carolina troops fire at each other.

Huckins spent most of the day visiting members of his church whose fathers, brothers, and sons were participating in the bombardment. That evening he wrote his daughter Mary, who was at school in the central part of the state, to inform her of the unique happenings of the day.

He described the firing and noted that "everybody was out" to see it, even her sister Sarah. He also told her that her mother had wished to go and see the action, but that he had forbidden it, especially since she had been sick in bed for three months. In describing the atmosphere of the city, Huckins said,

> Great anxiety prevails, but a strong determination with everyone to do his duty. The troops are crowding in by thousands. The city is strongly guarded. All the Fire companies are under arms, and three hundred gentlemen parade the city at night on horseback. All

the stores are closed. The north mail is suspended. The cars are not allowed to go farther on North Eastern R. [sic] road. No telegraphic dispatches are allowed to be sent, except by proper authorities. What tomorrow will bring to light no one knows.[24]

The firing continued as fiercely the next day, until a white flag hoisted at Fort Sumter that afternoon ended the contest. The following day, 14 June, United States forces were escorted from the fort.

During the almost four months between the adoption of the Ordinance of Secession and the firing on Fort Sumter, several other states had seceded and joined with South Carolina to form a confederacy. Now, as summer approached, the United States of America and the Confederate States of America mustered their forces to undertake what would become the bloodiest war the world had ever experienced.

In May, as the fever of hostilities continued to rise, Huckins and the other delegates to the eighth biennial session of the Southern Baptist Convention met at the First Baptist Church in Savannah. The convention patriotically supported Southern rights and elected a special Committee on the State of the Country. The committee recommended the adoption of resolutions vindicating the actions of the South in withdrawing from the Union and tendered the support of the denomination to the cause of the Confederacy.

This special committee also suggested that the convention pray fervently for the "friends, brothers, fathers, sons, and citizen soldiers, who have left their homes to go forth for the defence [sic] of their families and friends." In addition, it was suggested that the convention pray "for our enemies in the spirit of the Divine Master, who, 'When he was reviled, reviled not again...'"[25]

In anticipation of the usual consequences of war, the committee urged that the churches of the denomination

> observe the first and second days of June as days of humiliation, fasting, and prayer to the Almighty God,

that He may avert any calamities due to our sins as a people, and may look with mercy and favor upon us.[26]

During the next several weeks both the North and South hastened war preparations, calling for volunteers and mounting drives for recruits. By early July 1861, Federal forces were in Virginia, with the capture of the Confederate capital of Richmond as their objective. Rebel soldiers were rushed to its defense, resulting in the first major conflict between the two American armies. The Battle of Manassas on 21 July, ended in a rout of the Yankee troops. In retreat, they mingled with civilians who had come to picnic and watch the fight, causing a major panic and embarrassment to the North. News of the victory bolstered the South, but the harsh fighting and the almost five thousand combined casualties served to awaken both sides to the realities of war.

This Southern victory was on the minds of most of the participants at the South Carolina Baptist State Convention during the last week of July, but it did not dominate the proceedings. Instead, the convention delegates followed their normal routines receiving activity reports, conducting business, and listening to sermons. Among the speakers was James Huckins who exhorted the gathering to continue to support all the denomination's educational endeavors. He also spoke in favor of a proposal that recommended the convention establish its own newspaper. However, the time was not yet right for this idea, and the attempt failed.[27] After the convention, Huckins returned to Charleston, where activities aimed at "providing for our boys in camps, hospitals, and those preparing to go" were under way.[28]

In late April 1861, President Lincoln had proclaimed a blockade of Confederate ports from South Carolina to Texas. Although this measure was largely ineffective at first, gradually Union ships began appearing offshore near many of the Southern cities. On 4 July, the United States steamer *South Carolina* had arrived in Galveston Bay, causing many in the island city to flee for the mainland, including a large contingent of the members of the Galveston Baptist Church, which closed its doors.[29]

By early fall the blockade of Charleston's harbor was seriously interfering with the daily lives of the citizens of that city. Even though a few ships managed to slip by the Union frigates, the vast majority of shipping at the Charleston port had come to a halt. The result was a decrease in available supplies and a corresponding increase in prices. As far as possible people attempted to help each other, especially those within the same neighborhoods or members of the same churches, but gradually the deprivations began to affect the city profoundly.

Around the first of November, a menagerie of different kinds and sizes of Union ships landed on the southern shores of South Carolina. Troops from the ships methodically worked their way through Hilton Head Island, forcing the planters who lived along the shores to flee. In retaliation, the planters burned their much-needed cotton behind them.

When the Charleston Baptist Association convened on 16 November 1861, only eighteen delegates representing nine churches were present. The people in the city were so busy preparing for a possible invasion of Union forces that little time could be spared to a meeting of this nature. Although Huckins had the double responsibility of caring for his family and ministering to his congregation, he felt the business of the association was of such importance that it required his attendance.

At the meeting he was elected moderator *pro tem* and called upon to deliver the first sermon. Later, when he gave the report of his church, he seemed to be expressing the feelings of many people of South Carolina as he stated that they had been

> blest with a great degree of health the past season, owing to His kind providential care; and since He has kept us from the ravages of the pestilence, Shall we not trust Him to protect us from the still more dreadful ravages of the foe who is now invading our shores. Our God does not change; He is the same now, as when in ancient time, He so often preserved His chosen people from the designs of their adversaries, and we have every reason to trust that He will now hear the prayers of His people, and will save us from our foes.[30]

Huckins was requested by the delegates to draft the Circular Letter that was to be sent to other churches in the state. In it Huckins called the enemy "rapacious and bloodthirsty." He vowed to follow the example of the Revolutionary forefathers and "be bold of heart, and strong in the strength of the Lord of Hosts." He also reiterated the hope and confidence that the people of Charleston had "in the mighty arm of Jehovah," though the city was just beginning to feel the effects of the "most cruel war."[31]

He concluded the letter with words of encouragement and sympathy, writing

> We tender to you our tenderest sympathy in our common sufferings. Our fathers, brothers, and sons are fighting the same foe. They stand side by side. Some of them have already fallen, and more must fall. Let common dangers and grief bring our hearts to a closer fellowship and give more intensity to our love.[32]

Such undaunted confidence in God's safekeeping began to wane for many Charlestonians 11 December. That evening a small fire whipped by relentless winds became a roaring inferno that eventually destroyed a quarter of the city. Firemen fought all night as the people stood outside their houses helplessly watching the crimson glow shadow-dancing on the clouds above the city. Soldiers in camps surrounding Charleston begged for permission to leave to help fight the flames, but all such requests were denied. In spite of orders to the contrary, many soldiers broke out of their camps and rushed to the city, only to stare at the smouldering ruins of what they had known as their own.[33]

The next morning, as the sun cautiously peeked through the lingering smoke and haze, residents of the city were able to take stock of the immense devastation. More than five hundred homes had been destroyed, along with five historic churches and numerous businesses and commercial buildings.

In what might have been seen as a portent of the future, Institute Hall, where the Ordinance of Secession had been adopted only a year earlier, was now only a memory. The fire did not touch everything, but what it embraced it completely obliterated. By morning it had burned a 540-acre swath through the heart of the city.[34]

Many of those who had lost their homes in the fire were now reduced to the status of refugees, along with the hundreds of others who had rushed into the city during the Union invasion of Hilton Head Island. Added to this misery was the implementation the next week of the United States government's decision to sink granite-laden whaling ships outside the mouth of Charleston harbor in an attempt to prevent blockade running. When this "Stone Fleet" was sunk on 19 and 20 December, it pulled the noose of economic disaster tightly around the city.

Because of the growing devastation and disorder, it soon became evident that the civilian population was a burden in the military's attempt to conduct the war in the area. As a result, all noncombatants were requested to leave Charleston for safer quarters in other places in the state. Huckins's wife and daughter were among the many who left.

IN THE EARLY STAGES OF THE WAR, as soldiers began to gather in camps all over the South, little attention was given to their religious needs. When the oversight became apparent, calls went out to churches and benevolent organizations to help alleviate that condition. In South Carolina the Baptists attempted to meet the challenge through the Sunday School and Colportage division of the State Convention, which purchased and disseminated large quantities of reading materials to the troops.

In January 1862 Huckins joined in this effort and began delivering religious materials to troops stationed in and around Charleston. He also began visiting hospitals to minister to the many sick and wounded who were being brought into the city. These activities were very familiar to Huckins, who had been uniquely prepared by his past experiences in Galveston.

During the next several weeks the number of wounded arriving in Charleston increased rapidly as Southern forces experienced heavy casualties in Virginia. Hospitals quickly overflowed so numerous buildings were rented and partially renovated in order to provide emergency facilities. Field hospitals were set up in camps, and all available medical personnel worked around the clock to treat the hundreds of sick and wounded.

Almost daily Huckins visited the camps and hospitals around Charleston to distribute tracts, religious books, and New Testaments. He also provided spiritual counsel to those who desired it and attended to the burial of many who died. In addition, he worked in conjunction with various ladies' benevolent societies to provide food and clothing to the soldiers and helped coordinate the collection and delivery of the varieties of materials sent by people from all over the South for relief of the suffering.

When a request for new religious reading material was issued by the South Carolina Baptist Convention, Huckins answered by writing several tracts. His first, "Goodness Conquers," was intended to show that kindness is the great influence in religion—"the method by which God redeems man, and by which God's servants must bring the guilty to submit to the method of redemption." The tract revealed the philosophy of Huckins's own life, as he had constantly "sought by unaffected expression of his sympathy for the suffering, and by liberal and thoughtful supplies for the needy, to open their hearts to the Gospel which it was his chief object to proclaim."[35]

In late April 1862, as the threat of attack by Union forces appeared imminent, the remaining noncombatants were requested to leave the city. After the worship service at Wentworth Street church on the first Sunday in May, "the men and women wept like children, not expecting for months to come back, if ever, to their dear church."[36]

On 7 May, when Huckins wrote his youngest daughter Mary, who was still in school in Spartanburg, he described Charleston as a city in great distress, calling the scene "heart rending." As he told her of his constant visits to the sick within the city as well as in the camps and hospitals, he confessed he was growing weary. He also was worried about the future of Charleston. He wrote,

> I know not my dear child what may be before us, but sorrow I know and perhaps want. Charleston, if attacked within the next month is sure to fall. But if not till July, we may be able to defend the city.[37]

Huckins encouraged his daughter to pray that the Lord would "open some way whereby I may be able to support you and the family, or that he will open some way by which you and Sarah can support yourselves." He reminded her that "God will not leave us if we trust in Him with our whole hearts. Trouble should make us more gentle toward one another and toward everyone." In closing, he remarked, "The South may be killed, but conquered they will not be. They will be defiant even in death."[38]

When the State Convention met in Greenville in July, Huckins's pressing responsibilities in the camps and hospitals around Charleston kept him from participating. Because of prevailing conditions of hardship throughout the state, only forty-six delegates—about half the usual number—were able to attend.[39] Even though he was not present at the convention, the delegates there elected Huckins a trustee of Furman University and a delegate to the Southern Baptist Convention scheduled to meet in Columbus, Mississippi, in May 1863. His election as a trustee of Furman anticipated future peaceful times. The university had closed because of the war and was not expected to reopen until hostilities had ceased.[40]

Throughout the rest of the summer and into the fall, Huckins continued his daily ministrations in the hospitals and camps. He visited the soldiers, slept beside them upon the damp and musty straw, ate with them, read letters and religious materials to them, and prayed with them separately and in groups. He also visited other Baptist associations in the state to solicit money, clothing, food, and supplies for the troops.

During this time Huckins worked very closely with the doctors to procure the supplies they so badly needed. His constant pleas for assistance did not go unheeded as boxes and packages filled with medicines, clothing, and foodstuffs continually arrived from all over the South.

On 26 October 1862, Huckins wrote the editor of the newly established newspaper, *The Confederate Baptist*, and told of delivering a carpetbag of socks to the Roper Hospital, one of many in which he ministered. The socks "were gratefully appreciated," he said, and added, "A single pair of socks, or a warm flannel shirt, may save a valuable life." He also informed the editor of his fears that Charleston soon would come under attack and that "bandages and blankets will be then imperatively needed." He encouraged contributions from all the readers of the newspaper.[41]

Huckins's strenuous routine of daily rounds in the camps and hospitals did not prohibit him from ministering to the few members of the Wentworth Street church who still remained in the city, or from participating in denominational activities. On 15 November, Huckins gathered with a small number of ministers and laymen for the 111th session of the Charleston Association, at which he was elected moderator and preached the charity sermon. In his message he related "many touching incidents which drew tears from the audience and contributed much in eliciting the liberal amount which was offered for the soldiers."[42]

The report of the Wentworth Street church to the association indicated that eighteen people had been added to its rolls by baptism since the meeting the previous year. In addition, several sons of the church members had been led to Christ by Huckins while they were stationed in camps near the city.[43]

In the Circular Letter that Huckins wrote on behalf of the association, he described the distressing conditions within and around Charleston stating that

> The loss of membership incurred by battle and disease has been fearful; nearly every church is in mourning, and we fear that the desire for the removal of these calamities has been stronger than the revival of pure religion. . . . We greatly fear that the hearts of our members are not sufficiently humbled before God. May the Lord bring us speedily to his feet and may this disastrous eclipse of our religious and political prosperity soon pass off, and the son of righteousness and peace shine out upon us in unveiled glory.[44]

Huckins noted that although some of the churches "were nearly broken up by the dispersion of their members, and some had lost their all for this world," contributions had increased.[45] The needs of the war seemed to open wide the pocketbooks of the Baptists in and around Charleston.

16

AS THE END OF 1862 NEARED, the plight of the South appeared grave. Very few victories had been won by the Confederates, and the Union forces had captured several important Southern cities. Evidences of impending disaster continued to mount. In Charleston the blockade had successfully shut down all shipping. Frequent shelling from Union ships on the city's fortifications kept the South Carolina troops on alert and the remaining citizens on the edge of panic.

Soldiers in the camps, as well as the wounded and sick in the hospitals, continually sought ease from the pangs of war by reading any printed material that became available to them. Newspapers were precious commodities. Although only a few were circulated in the Charleston area, these were read and reread until the pages became almost too thin to turn. Religious newspapers often contained news of the war, so the soldiers eagerly perused these publications as well as the secular ones.

In January 1863, Huckins was appointed a colporteur and missionary to hospitals by the South Carolina Baptist Convention. He had been engaged in this type of endeavor for almost a year, delivering Bibles, tracts, and other printed material to soldiers in the camps and hospitals, but now the convention was going to pay him fifty dollars per month for his efforts.

Because of his close association with the soldiers and his involvement with the military establishment, Huckins felt that he could minister more effectively to the troops if he were one of them. Thus, in February he applied for appointment as a chaplain in the Confederate Army. A month later he was commissioned a chaplain with the rank of captain and a salary of approximately twenty-eight dollars per month.[1]

Although Huckins appeared to be doing all that was humanly possible as he ministered to the sick and wounded, distributed literature, preached to the soldiers, visited the prisons to witness to both Northern and Southern troops, arranged funerals, and notified families of the conditions of their loved ones, his commission seemed to confer upon him an additional burst of energy. He quickened his pace, often spending whole nights in the hospitals moving from cot to cot to pray and talk with the sick. Then without any sleep, he would frequently work the next day to share the love of Christ by word and example. Though he was spreading himself too thin and neglecting his own physical needs, he was excited about his work. Huckins believed that God's grace was the "true leaven" that could solve the problems that arose between men.

Because he was so interested in the spiritual welfare of the soldiers, he attempted to nurture their souls by providing as much physical comfort as he could muster under the circumstances. He collected money, eggs, chickens, dried fruit, hospital supplies, socks, blankets, bandages, coffee, tea, flour, cornmeal, lard, butter, and anything else that he could persuade people to donate. He always found a use for what people gave to "his" soldiers.

Frequently the troops in the camps formed prayer meetings, and Huckins tried to attend many of these.[2] He preached almost every day or night, and the soldiers were always glad to hear him. "His sermons unanimously engaged serious attention, while profound silence and deep solemnity prevailed."[3] When he had the opportunity to baptize new converts, he usually tried to use the occasion to share the Gospel with those gathered to witness the ceremony.

At the meeting of the State Convention held during the last week of July 1863, Huckins told the delegates of the continuing needs of the soldiers and requested their support. They immediately contributed $127, making the total that Huckins had collected during the almost eighteen months in which he had ministered to the soldiers more than $6,500—a remarkable feat in a time of such devastation and despair.

On 5 August, a week after returning from the meeting of the State Convention, Huckins requested a sixty-day furlough. He was tired and weary, his health had degenerated greatly, and his eyesight was almost gone. He found that "having become very much impaired" he was unable to perform his duties to the extent he wished.[4] He wrote to his wife who had moved to the interior of the state, that he was coming to see her, though he "would give millions to stay and labor where he was."[5]

That afternoon and evening as he visited with the soldiers in the hospitals, the humid Charleston weather gradually sapped his remaining strength. Regardless, he continued going from bed to bed visiting those who needed him. On through the night he ministered to the suffering, giving no consideration to his own needs.

The morning sun was a welcome sight to Huckins's weary body. Though he had fever and needed to lie down, he continued to work, even making arrangements for others to supply the hospitals while he was on furlough.

Then he sought rest—but only for a little while, as he planned on leaving later that day of 6 August to see his wife. He closed his eyes to seek refreshment in slumber. He was tired, worn, and thin. He rested—he richly deserved it. It was a rest from which he never awoke.

The next day his body was buried beside a giant oak tree in Charleston's Magnolia Cemetery. His task was completed. He died as he had lived—in the service of Jesus Christ—and for James Huckins, there was nothing better than this.

Notes

Chapter 1

1. Henry Winthrop Hardon, "Huckins Family, A Reprint with Corrections and Considerable Additions," *The New England Historical and Genealogical Register, 1913–1915* (Privately Printed, 1916), 28–29.

2. S. C. Griffin, *History of Galveston* (Galveston: A. H. Cawston, 1931), 135–37.

3. Wilbur LaFayette, *Early History of Vermont*, vol. 4 (Jericho, Vt.: Roscoe Printing House, 1903), 406–7.

4. *Minutes of the Woodstock Association, Held at Newport, New Hampshire, September 27–28, 1826* (Simeon Ide., 1825), n.p.

5. *Historical Sketch of the New Hampton Institution, New Hampton, N. H.* (Bristol, N. H.: R. W. Musgrove, 1876), 5–6.

6. *Minutes, Boston Baptist Association, Held at the First Baptist Meeting House in Charlestown on Wednesday and Thursday, September 19 & 20, 1827, being its Sixteenth Anniversary* (Boston: Lincoln & Edmands, 1827), 17.

7. *Catalogue of the Members of the Literary Adelphi of the Academical and Theological Institution at New Hampton, New Hampshire* (Concord: Morrill, Silsby and Co., 1844), 2, 9.

8. *Catalogue of the Officers and Students of the Academic and Theological Institution, New Hampton, N. H.* (Concord: N. H.: R. H. Sherburne & Co., 1829), 18–19.

9. Grenville Meller, ed., *A Book of the United States Exhibiting its Geography, Divisions, Constitution and Government* (Hartford: H. F. Sumner & Co., 1838), 323–24.

10. "James Huckins," registrar materials, Brown University, Providence, R. I.

11. J. S. Buckingham, *America, Historical, Statistic and Descriptive*, vol. 3 (London: Fisher, Son and Co., 1841), 473–75.

12. Ibid.

13. *Triennial Catalogue of the Library and the Members of the Philermenian Society in Brown University. Founded A. D. 1795* (Providence, R. I., 1849), 5–8.

14. *Minutes of the 43rd Anniversary of the State Convention of the Baptist Denomination in South Carolina, Held at Darlington, July 24th to 27th, 1863, and at Greenville, July 29 to Aug. 1, 1864* (Columbia, S. C.: F. G. DeFontaine & Co., 1864), 202.

15. Information about engagement can be found in letter from John B. Barton to his daughter, Emeline, dated 9 April 1832. Typescript of this letter is in The Texas Collection, Baylor University, Waco, Texas. For information on General Barton see Mrs. Catherine R. Williams, *Biography of Revolutionary Heroes; Containing the Life of Brigadier Gen. William Barton, and also, of Captain Stephen Olney* (Providence: Published by the author, 1839).

16. *List of the Members of the First Baptist Church in Providence with Biographical Sketches of the Pastors* (Providence: H. H. Brown, 1832), n.p.

17. Lilley Eaton, *Genealogical History of the Town of Reading, Mass. including the present towns of Wakefield, Reading, and North Reading with Chronological and Historical Sketches, from 1639 to 1874* (Boston: Alfred Mudge & Son, Printers, 1874), 207.

18. John Warner Barber, *Massachusetts Historical Collection* (Worchester: Dorr, Howland & Co., 1839), 427.

19. W. H. Eaton, *Historical Sketch of the Massachusetts Baptist Missionary Society and Convention, 1802–1902* (Boston: Massachusetts Baptist Convention, 1903), 4–7, 50–54.

20. Rev. N. R. Everts, *History of the First Baptist Church in Wakefield, Mass., 1800–1900* (Malden: G. E. Dunbar, 1901), 27–29.

21. J. M. Allen, *The United States Baptist Annual Register and Almanac*, vol. 1 (Philadelphia, 1823), 70.

22. "Minutes of the First Baptist Church" (Andover, Mass.), 21 September 1832, 1.

23. John Warner Barber, *Historical Collections Being a General Collection of Interesting Facts, Traditions, Biographical Sketches, Anecdotes, etc. Relating to the History and Antiquities of Every Town in Massachusetts with Geographical Descriptions* (Worcester: Warren Lazell, 1848), 160–62.

24. Document, Commonwealth of Massachusetts, 28 February 1835, Andover, Massachusetts.

25. J. R. Stevenson, historian, First Baptist Church, Andover, to Eugene W. Baker, 21 July 1983, quoting from a sermon delivered in 1902 by Rev. Arthur T. Belknap, fourteenth minister of the First Baptist Church, Andover, copy in Baylor University Historian papers, The Texas Collection, Baylor University, Waco, Texas (hereafter cited as Texas Collection).

26. I. C. Knowlton, *Annals of Calais, Maine and St. Stephen, New Brunswick: Including the Village of Milltown, ME., and the Present town of Milltown, N. B.* (Calais: J. A. Sears, Printer, 1875), 47.

27. Ibid., 50.

28. Ibid., 137.

29. *Minutes of the Maine Baptist Convention, 12th Anniversary, Holden in Bangor, October 5th and 6th, 1836* ([Portland]: Charles Day and Co., Printers, 1836), 40.

30. William Cathcart, *Baptist Encyclopedia* (Philadelphia: Louis H. Everts, 1881), 1067.

31. Knowlton, *Annals*, 173.

32. James Huckins Papers, Texas Collection.

33. Knowlton, *Annals*, 135.

34. Mary Burnham Putnam, *The Baptists and Slavery, 1840–1845* (Ann Arbor, Mich.: Charles Wahr, 1913), 17–18.

35. Chester W. Eaton and Warren E. Eaton, eds., *Proceedings of the 250th Anniversary of the Ancient Town of Redding [sic]* (Reading, Mass.: Loring & Twombly, 1896), 246.

36. *Minutes of the Fiftieth Session of the Salem Baptist Association Held with the First Baptist Church in Beverly, October 10 and 11, 1877* (Boston: J. M. Hewes, 1877), 19–20.

37. Putnam, *Baptists and Slavery*, 8–10.

38. Robert A. Baker, *Relations Between Northern and Southern Baptists* (Fort Worth, 1948), 43–44.

39. Richard O. Curry, *The Abolitionists, Reformers or Fanatics?* (New York: Holt, Rinehart and Winston, 1965), 21.

40. Putnam, *Baptists and Slavery*, 16.

41. *Minutes of the Maine Baptist Convention, Held at Waterville, October 3 & 4, 1838* (Brunswick: T. W. Newman, 1838), n.p.

42. Knowlton, *Annals*, 138.

43. Ibid., 139.

44. *The Christian Index*, 14 March 1839.

45. James Huckins to his wife, 29 December 1838, from Savannah, Ga., copy in Texas Collection.

46. Ibid.

47. Ibid.

48. Ibid.

49. Cathcart, *Baptist Encyclopedia*, 779–81.

50. C. D. Mallary, *Memoirs of Elder Jesse Mercer* (New York: Lewis Colby, 1844), 169.

51. *The Christian Index*, 7 February 1839.

52. Huckins to wife, 29 December 1838, copy in Texas Collection.

53. Z. N. Morrell, *Flowers and Fruits from the Wilderness, or Thirty-Six Years in Texas and Two Winters in Honduras* (1872; reprint, Waco, Tex.: The Markham Press Fund of Baylor University Press, 1976), 20.

54. J. B. Link, ed., *Texas Historical and Biographical Magazine*, vol. 1 (Austin: 1891), 391–93.

55. J. M. Carroll, *A History of Texas Baptists* (Dallas: Baptist Standard Publishing Co., 1923), 137–39.

56. *The Baptist Advocate*, New York, 6 July 1839; also *The Seventh Report of the Executive Committee of the American Baptist Home Mission Society, presented at its Anniversary in Philadelphia, April 26, 1839 with the Treasurer's Report* (New York: Mission Rooms, 1839), 29.

57. *Eighteen Anniversary of the Georgia Baptist Convention, Held at Richland, Twiggs County, Geo. On the 3d, 4th & 6th days of May, 1839* (Washington: M. J. Kappel at the Office of *The Christian Index*, 1839), 4.

58. William B. Sprague, *Annals of the American Pulpit or Commemorative Notices of Distinguished American Clergymen of Various Denominations* (New York: Robert Carter & Brothers, 1860), 812.

59. *The Christian Index*, 25 December 1920, quoting Jesse Mercer to Dr. Brantley, 13 February 1833.

60. There is no definite evidence that the William Tryon who emigrated to Texas in December 1835 is the same William M. Tryon who went to Texas in 1841. However, because of the similarity of the names, it is assumed that these are the same person. See records in General Land Office, Austin, Texas, "Republic Texas, County Jasper, Town Zavala," 10 May 1836.

61. *Minutes of the 15th Anniversary of the Georgia Baptist Convention, Held at Talbottom, Georgia on the 29th & 30th April and 2nd & 3rd of May, 1836*, 6; also "Georgia Baptist Convention Executive Committee," 2 May 1836, Archives, Mercer University, Macon, Ga.

62. "Minutes, Eufaula Baptist Church," 22 July 1837, 23 September 1837, Samford University library, Birmingham, Ala. (At the time of Tryon's pastorate, the name of the town was Irwinton. It was later changed to Eufaula.)

63. *The Christian Index*, 12 December 1839, quoting James Huckins to Jesse Mercer, 29 November 1839.

64. *The Baptist Advocate*, 7 December 1839.

65. Ibid.

66. James Huckins to wife, 15 November 1839 from New York, copy in Texas Collection.

67. *The Baptist Advocate*, 2 February 1840, quoting from David Wright to his father, 28 November 1839 and 2 December 1839.

68. Ibid.

69. *Minutes of the State Convention of the Baptist Denomination in South Carolina at its 19th Anniversary, Held at the Black Swamp Church, Beaufort District, December 7th and continued to December 10th, 1839*, 3–4.

70. Carroll, *A History*, 142.

71. Ibid.

72. Ibid.

73. H. H. Furman to Judge B. C. Franklin, 21 January 1840, Texas State Archives, Austin.

74. Walter Prescott Webb, ed., *The Handbook of Texas*, vol. 1 (Austin: The Texas State Historical Association, 1952), 640.

75. Carroll, *A History*, 143.

76. Ibid.

77. Charles Hooton, *St. Louis Isle or Texiana with Additional Observations Made in the United States and in Canada* (London: Simmons and Ward, 1847), 7.

78. Sam P. Graham, ed., *Galveston Community Book* (Galveston: Arthur H. Cawston, 1945), 8.

79. Ibid.

80. William Kennedy, *Texas: The Rise, Progress and Prospects of the Republic of Texas*, vol. 2 (London: R. Hastings, 1841), 407–8.

81. Hooton, *St. Louis Isle*, 11.

Chapter 2

1. Carroll, *A History*, 143.

2. Ibid.

3. Joe B. Frantz, *Gail Borden, Dairyman to a Nation* (Norman, Okla.: University of Oklahoma Press, 1951), 164.

4. Carroll, *A History*, 145–46.

5. *The Christian Index*, 24 September 1840.

6. Ibid.

7. Ibid.

8. "Minutes, Galveston Baptist Church," 30 January 1840.

9. Ibid.

10. Carroll, *A History*, 144.

11. Nina Brown Baker, *Texas Yankee, The Story of Gail Borden* (New York: Harcourt, Brace and Co., 1955), 37.

12. Robert E. Davis, ed., *The Diary of William Barrett Travis, August 39, 1833–June 26, 1834* (Waco: Texian Press, 1972), explanatory note, 26.

13. Charles W. Haynes, *History of the Island and the City of Galveston*, vol. 2 (Cincinnati, 1879), 834–39.

14. Carroll, *A History*, 146.

15. Ibid.

16. Ibid., 147.

17. *The Christian Index*, 1 October 1840.

18. Carroll, *A History*, 147.

19. Morrell, *Flowers and Fruits*, 66.

20. *The Christian Index*, 14 May 1840.

21. Ibid.

22. Ibid.

23. *The Christian Index*, 8 October 1840.

24. Ibid.

25. Ibid.

26. *The Christian Index*, 15 October 1840.

27. Ibid.

28. Mary Wharton Malthy to General Carvajal in New Orleans, undated, Archives, Louisiana State University Library. Mary Malthy was a niece of R. E. B. Baylor. See also Sam Houston Dixon and Louis Wiltz Kemp, *The Heroes of San Jacinto* (Houston: The Anson Jones Press, 1932), 378.

29. R. E. B. Baylor to J. H. Stribling, 13 April 1871, from Holly Oak, Texas Collection.

30. "Minutes, Good Hope Baptist Church, Talledega, Alabama, 1836–1840," Microfilm, Samford University library, Birmingham.

31. Carroll, *A History*, 156.

32. Ibid., 156–57.

33. James Huckins to S. H. Cone quoted in *The Baptist Advocate*, 27 June 1840.

34. *The Eighth Report of the American Baptist Home Mission Society, Presented by the Executive Committee at the Anniversary in New York, April 28, 1840 with the Treasurer's Report* (New York: Mission Rooms, 1840), 4.

35. Ibid., 25.

36. "Minutes, Wetumpka Baptist Church, Wetumpka, Alabama, 1839–40," n.p.

37. Rhoda Barton Huckins to her sister, Emeline, Buffalo, New York, 8 September 1840, copy in Texas Collection.

38. "Executive Committee Minutes, American Baptist Home Mission Society," 3 November 1840. Quoted in Lily Russell research materials, Texas Collection.

39. Rhoda Barton Huckins to her sister, Emeline, 8 September 1840, copy in Texas Collection.

40. George H. Hansell, *Reminiscences of Baptist Churches and Baptist Leaders in New York City and Vicinity, From 1835–1898* (New York: American Baptist Publication Society, 1899), 21.

41. Carroll, *A History*, 141.

Chapter 3

1. *The Ninth Report of the American Baptist Home Mission Society presented by the Executive Committee at the Anniversary in Baltimore, April 27, 1841* (New York: Mission Rooms, 1841), 25.

2. "Passengers Lists, Port of Galveston," 30 December 1840, Texas State Archives, Austin. *The Christian Index*, 28 May 1841, quoting an article that had appeared in *The Baptist Advocate*.

3. "Minutes, Galveston Baptist Church," 27 March 1841.

4. "Records of the First Baptist Church in Houston," 10 April 1841, copy at A. Webb Roberts Library, Southwestern Baptist Theological Seminary, Fort Worth, Texas.

5. "Minutes, Galveston Baptist Church," 22 May 1841.

6. Robert A. Baker, *The Blossoming Desert, A Concise History of Texas Baptists* (Waco, Tex.: Word Books, 1970), 61–63.

7. Morrell, *Flowers and Fruits*, 132.

8. Baker, *Blossoming Desert*, 74–76.

9. Morrell, *Flowers and Fruits*, 144–45.

10. *Minutes of the Second Annual Session of the Union Baptist Association Held at the Clear Creek Meeting House Near Rutersville in Western Texas, Commencing on the 7th October, A. D. 1841*, 23.

11. Ibid., 24–25; *The Eleventh Report of the American Baptist Home Mission Society presented by the Executive Committee at the Anniversary in Albany, N.Y., April 25, 1843* (New York: Mission Rooms, 1843), 35.

12. *Minutes of the Second Annual Session of the Union Baptist Association...*, 23–24; Harry Haynes, *The Life and Writings of Rufus C. Burleson* (Compiled and Published by Mrs. Georgia J. Burleson, 1901), 186.

13. *The Christian Index*, 21 January 1842, quoting extracts James Huckins to Benjamin Hill, 14 November 1841.

14. *Minutes of the Second Annual Session of the Union Baptist Association*, 25.

15. Morrell, *Flowers and Fruits*, 147.

Chapter 4

1. Walter Prescott Webb, ed., *The Handbook of Texas*, vol. 2 (Austin: The Texas State Historical Association, 1952), 729.

2. T. R. Fehrenbach, *Lone Star, A History of Texas and the Texans* (New York: Macmillan Co., 1968), 261.

3. Carroll, *A History*, 182.

4. *The Christian Index*, 15 April 1842, quoting letter from James Huckins, 11 March 1842.

5. Ibid.

6. *Baptist Banner and Western Pioneer*, 30 June 1842.

7. Ibid.

8. Ibid.

9. *Baptist Banner and Western Pioneer*, 18 August 1842.

10. Joseph Milton Nance, *Attack and Counter-Attack, The Texas-Mexican Frontier, 1842* (Austin: University of Texas Press, 1964), 342.

11. *The Christian Index*, 28 April 1843.

12. *Minutes of the Third Annual Session of the Union Baptist Association*, 1843, 4.

13. *The Christian Index*, 28 April 1843.

14. Ibid.

15. Ibid.

16. Link, *Texas Hist. and Bio. Magazine* 1:189.

17. *The Texas Baptist*, 14 November 1855.

18. Ibid.

19. Link, *Texas Hist. and Bio. Magazine* 1:186.

20. Gail Borden, Jr., to Executive Committee, American Baptist Home Mission Society, 5 March 1843, quoted in "Minutes, Galveston Baptist Church."

21. Ibid.

22. Charles W. Hayes, *History of the Island and the City of Galveston* (Cincinnati, 1879), 476.

23. Graham, *Galveston Comm. Book*, 19.

24. Putnam, *Baptists and Slavery*, 21.

25. Link, *Texas Hist. and Bio. Magazine* 1:189.

26. *Thirteenth Report of the American Baptist Home Mission Society presented by the Executive Board at the Anniversary at Providence, Rhode Island, April 29, 1845* (New York: Baptist Home Mission Rooms, 1845), 45.

27. Baylor to Stribling, 13 April 1871.

28. Haynes, *Life and Writings of Burleson*, 127.

29. Link, *Texas Hist. and Bio. Magazine* 1:188.

Chapter 5

1. Link, *Texas Hist. and Bio. Magazine* 1:188.

2. Morrell, *Flowers and Fruits*, 137.

3. *Minutes of the Fourth Anniversary Meeting of the Union Baptist Association convened at Providence Church, Washington County, October 6, 1843 and Days Following* (Washington: Thomas Johnson, Printers, 1843), 6.

4. *Minutes of the First Session of the Union Baptist Association Begun and Held in the Town of Travis in Western Texas, Oct. 8th, 1840* (Houston: Telegraph Press, 1840), reprint, 6–7.

5. Several excellent discussions relating to the possible founding dates of the Texas Baptist Education Society are found in Link, *Texas Hist. and Bio. Magazine* 1:44; Carroll, *A History*, 228–29; Haynes, *Life and Writings of Burleson*, 100–101; Morrell, *Flowers and Fruits*, 133, 138; Baker, *Blossoming Desert*, 81–83; B. F. Fuller, *History of Texas Baptists* (Louisville, Ky.: Baptist Book Concern, 1900), 120–21. The year 1841 is selected as the date of the society's establishment, primarily because of James Huckins's letter of 14 November 1841 to the American Baptist Home Mission Society in which he indicates that such a society had been established.

6. Baker, *Blossoming Desert*, 83.

7. R. E. B. Baylor correspondence, undated and unaddressed, Texas Collection.

8. *Baptist Banner and Western Pioneer*, 18 August 1842.

9. Haynes, *Life and Writings of Burleson*, 101.

10. Baylor correspondence, undated and unaddressed, Texas Collection.

11. R. E. B. Baylor to James Huckins, 1 March 1859, Texas Collection.

12. Carroll, *A History*, 229–30.

13. Baylor University Charter, copy in Texas Collection; original in Texas State Archives, Austin.

14. "Minutes, Galveston Baptist Church," 9 March 1845.

15. Ibid., 16 March 1845.

16. Ibid.

17. Gail Borden to Executive Committee, American Baptist Home Mission Society, 25 March 1845, quoted in "Minutes, Galveston Baptist Church."

Chapter 6

1. Gail Borden to Reverend Basil Manly, 2 July 1845, quoted in "Minutes, Galveston Baptist Church."

2. Ibid.

3. Borden to Manly, 22 March 1846, quoted in "Minutes, Galveston Baptist Church."

4. Ibid.

5. "Minutes, Galveston Baptist Church," 10 April 1846.

6. "Minutes, Executive Committee, Georgia Baptist Convention," 16 March 1846, Mercer University Archives, Macon, Ga.

7. "Minutes, Galveston Baptist Church," 10 April 1846.

8. This probably was the Galveston Academy of Huckins.

9. "Minutes, Galveston Baptist Church," 10 April 1846.

10. *Proceedings of the First Triennial Meeting of the Southern Baptist Convention, Held at Richmond, Virginia, June 10, 11, 12, 13, and 15, 1846* (Richmond H. K. Ellyson, 1846), 49–53.

11. Ibid.

12. Carroll, *A History*, 230.

13. "Minutes, Galveston Baptist Church," 24 July 1846.

14. Robert Selph Henry, *The Story of the Mexican War* (New York: The Bobbs-Merrill Company, Inc., 1950), 17

15. Huckins to his wife, 11 July 1846, copy in Texas Collection.

16. Ibid.

17. Ibid.

18. "Minutes, Galveston Baptist Church," 24 July 1846.

19. "Minutes, Galveston Baptist Church," 2 August 1846.

20. "Minutes, Galveston Baptist Church," 7 August 1846.

Chapter 7

1. *The Southern Baptist Missionary Journal*, 1, no. 6 (November 1846): 139.

2. Ibid.

3. *Minutes of the Seventh Annual Meeting of the Union Baptist Association Held with the Dove Church, Caldwell, Burleson County, on the 1st day of October, 1846 and days following*, 1.

4. Ibid., 2–3.

5. Ibid., 4.

6. "Baylor University Board of Trustee Minutes," Independence, 8 October 1846, 28, Texas Collection.

7. Ibid.

8. Arthur A. Grusendorf, "A Century of Education in Washington County, Texas." This is an article revised from the author's unpublished Ph. D. dissertation "The Social and Philosophical Determinants of Education in Washington County since 1835" (University of Texas, Austin, 1938), quoting the *Texas Republican*, Brazoria, 13 December 1834, 52.

9. Frances Trask to her father, Israel Trask, 5 July 1835, copy in Trask Papers, Archives, University of Texas.

10. H. P. N. Gammel, *The Laws of Texas*, vol. 1 (Austin: The Gammel Book Company, 1898), 1295–96.

11. *Texas Telegraph and Register*, 29 May 1839.

12. Webb, ed., *Texas Handbook* 1:876.

13. The bids were in land and property. To evaluate comparatively that which was offered, the trustees established a price of seventy-five cents per acre on all uncultivated land and set all property value at the estimated cost it would bring in a cash sale. Based on this calculation the land and property submitted by Independence was valued at $7,925. The bid of Huntsville totaled $5,417.75 and Shannon's Prairie was $4,725. The offer of Travis amounted to $3,586.25. "Baylor Trustee Minutes," 8 October 1846, 10.

14. "Baylor Trustee Minutes," 12 January 1846, 14.

15. Link, *Texas Hist. and Bio. Magazine* 2:50.

16. Arthur A. Grusendorf, "Henry F. Gillette—Baylor's First Teacher," *The Baylor Line*, March–April 1968, 26–28.

17. "Baylor Trustee Minutes," 12 January 1846, 29.

18. *The Southern Baptist Missionary Journal*, November 1846, 140.

19. *The Southern Baptist Missionary Journal*, March 1847, 235.

20. *The Southern Baptist Missionary Journal*, November 1846, 140.

21. Link, *Texas Hist. and Bio. Magazine* 1:203.

22. Link, *Texas Hist. and Bio. Magazine* 2:50; also *General Catalogue* [Colgate University], vol. 1 (Hamilton, [New York], 1937), 48.

Chapter 8

1. *The Southern Baptist Missionary Journal*, July 1847, 49–50.

2. Ibid.

3. Ibid.

4. Ibid.

5. Ibid.

6. Ibid.

7. *The Southern Baptist Missionary Journal*, September 1847, 98–99.

8. *The Christian Index*, 19 August 1847.

9. Ibid.

10. "Minutes, Galveston Baptist Church," 2 July 1847.

11. Ibid.

12. *The Southern Baptist Missionary Journal*, August 1847, 74.

13. "Minutes, Galveston Baptist Church," 12 September 1847.

14. Ibid., 20 November 1847.

15. Ibid.

16. Ibid.

17. Ibid.

18. Ibid.

19. Ibid.

20. *Minutes of the Eighth Annual Meeting of the Union Baptist Association Held with the First Baptist Church in Houston, Texas Commencing on Thursday, September 20 and Ending October 4, 1847*, 6.

21. Haynes, *Life and Writings of Burleson*, 186.

22. *Minutes of the Eighth Annual Meeting of the Union Baptist Association*, 6.

23. Ibid., 7.

24. *The Civilian and Galveston Gazette*, 20 November 1847.

25. *South Western Baptist Chronicle*, 27 November 1847.

26. *The Southern Baptist Missionary Journal*, January 1848, 193.

27. "Baylor Trustee Minutes," 22 December 1847, 37.

28. Ibid., 13 January 1846, 16.

29. Ibid., 4 February 1847, 31.

30. Ibid.

Chapter 9

1. *The Southern Baptist Missionary Journal*, September 1848, 95.

2. "Baylor Trustee Minutes," 1 June 1848, 40.

3. Ibid., 42.

4. Ibid., 43–44.

5. Ibid., 43.

6. *The Southern Baptist Missionary Journal,* April 1849, 258–60.

7. *Organization and Proceedings of the Baptist State Convention of Texas, Held with the Antioch Church, Anderson, Grimes County, September 8–12* (Huntsville: Banner Print, 1848), 10.

8. *Minutes of the Ninth Anniversary of the Union Baptist Association Held with the Independence Church, Washington Co., Texas, Commencing Sept. 28, and ending Oct. 2, 1848,* 3.

9. "Baylor Trustee Minutes," 2 April 1849, 46–50.

10. *Proceedings of the First Anniversary of the Baptist State Convention of Texas Held in the city of Houston, May 11–14, 1849,* n.p. n.d., 2–4.

11. Ibid., 4.

12. *The Southern Baptist Missionary Journal,* September 1849, 116.

13. "Baylor Trustee Minutes," 21 August 1849, 55.

Chapter 10

1. "Baylor Trustee Minutes," 13 June 1850, 57.

2. Link, *Texas Hist. and Bio. Magazine* 2:434.

3. "Baylor Trustee Minutes," 13 June 1851, 67.

4. Ibid., 14 June 1851, 67.

5. Ibid., 17 June 1851, 69.

6. "Minutes, First Baptist Church, Houston," 2 September 1850, copy at A. Webb Roberts Library.

7. Lois Smith Murray, *Baylor at Independence* (Waco, Tex.: Baylor University Press, 1972), 104–5.

8. "Baylor Trustee Minutes," 13 December 1851, 79–80.

9. *South Western Baptist,* 6 January 1852.

10. "Baylor Trustee Minutes," 22 January 1852, 84.

11. *The Southern Baptist Home Mission Journal,* June 1849, 21.

12. *South Western Baptist,* 18 February 1852.

13. Ibid.

14. Haynes, *Life and Writings of Burleson,* 124.

15. Ibid.

16. *Minutes of the Fifth Annual Session of the Baptist State Convention of Texas, Held at Marshall, in June, 1852* (Washington: *Lone Star* Office, 1852), 3, 10.

17. Ibid., 10–11.

18. Ibid., 11.

19. Ibid.

20. Ibid., 12.

21. "Baylor Trustee Minutes," 13 December 1851, 79.

22. *Minutes of the Fifth Annual Session of the Baptist State Convention,* 7.

23. "Baylor Trustee Minutes," 16 December 1852, 93.

24. Link, *Texas Hist. and Bio. Magazine* 1:167.

25. "Minutes, Galveston Baptist Church," 19 May 1853.

26. Huckins to J. P. Cole, 23 June 1853, recorded in "Minutes, Galveston Baptist Church."

27. Ibid.

28. Ibid.

29. "Baylor Trustee Minutes," 5 July 1853, 95.

Chapter 11

1. Peggy Hildreth, "The Howard Association of Galveston: The 1850s, Their Peak Years," *East Texas Historical Journal,* 17, no. 2 (1979), 37.

2. *The Confederate Baptist,* 2 September 1863.

3. Letter of "The First Baptist Church of Galveston to the Union Baptist Association," undated, "Minutes, Galveston Baptist Church."

4. "Howard Association of Galveston: 1854-1882," Minutes of 9 May 1854, Rosenberg Library, Galveston.

5. *Minutes of the Seventh Annual Session of the Baptist State Convention, of Texas. Held at Palestine, Anderson County, In June, 1854* (Anderson, Texas: Printed at the "Central Texian" Office, 1854), 15.

6. Ibid., 21.

7. Ibid., 3.

Chapter 12

1. For additional information on the articles of James Huckins, see *The Texas Baptist,* April-August 1851.

2. J. P. Cole to Gail Borden, Jr., in New York, 11 March 1855, Rosenberg Library, Galveston.

3. Cole to Borden, 15 April 1855, Rosenberg Library.

4. W. & D. Richardson, *Galveston Directory for 1859-60: With a Brief History of the Island Prior to the Foundation of the City* (Galveston: *News* Book and Job Office, 1859), 71.

5. Cole to Borden, 18 May 1855, Rosenberg Library.

6. *Minutes of the Sixteenth Annual Meeting of the Union Baptist Association Held with New Year's Creek Church, at Brenham, Washington County, Texas, Commencing Oct. 5, and closing Oct. 8, 1855* (Galveston: *Civilian* Book and Job Office, 1855), 3-11.

7. Ibid., 7, 8.

8. Cole to Borden, 15 April 1855, Rosenberg Library.

9. *Minutes of the Eighth Annual Session of the Baptist State Convention of the State of Texas, Held at Independence, Washington County, in November, 1855* (Anderson, Texas: *Texas Baptist* Office, 1855), 14.

10. Ibid., 4.

Chapter 13

1. *Proceedings of the Baptist State Convention Held with the Church in Anderson on Saturday Before the Fourth Sabbath in October, 1856* (Anderson, Tex.: Office of *The Texas Baptist,* 1856), 34–35.

2. *Minutes of the 17th Annual Session of the Union Baptist Association held with Laurel Hill Church at Cold Spring, Polk County, Texas, Commencing October 3d and Closing October 6th, 1856* (Anderson, Tex.: Office of *The Texas Baptist,* 1856), 6.

3. Ibid.

4. Ibid., 7.

5. *Proceedings of the Baptist State Convention held with the Church in Anderson on Saturday before the Fourth Sabbath in October, 1856,* 14, 18, 22, 27.

6. Ibid., 35–35.

Chapter 14

1. *South Western Baptist,* 9 April 1857.

2. Ibid.

3. *Minutes of the 18th Annual Session of the Union Baptist Association held with Bethany Church, Grimes County, Texas* (Anderson, Tex.: Office of *The Texas Baptist,* 1857), 7.

4. *Proceedings of the Baptist State Convention held with the Huntsville Baptist Church, Commencing on Saturday, October 24, 1857* (Anderson, Tex.: *The Texas Baptist,* 1857), 12.

5. Ibid., 11.

6. Ibid.

7. Ibid.

8. Ibid., 12.

9. Huckins to his wife, 18 July 1846. See also Galveston County Deed Records, 28 May 1848 (selling of two slaves); 26 April 1856 (purchase of a slave for $1,000).

10. "Minutes, Galveston Baptist Church," January 1859.

11. Ibid.

12. George Fellows to Bro. Sawyer, October 1844, Rosenberg Library.

Chapter 15

1. *Minutes of the 108th Session of the Charleston Baptist Association held with the Congaree Baptist Church, November 19–22, 1859* (Charleston, 1860), 10.

2. *Manual of the Citadel Square Baptist Church* (Charleston, S.C., 1880), n.p.

3. *Charleston Courier*, 29 October 1859; 5 November 1859; 12 November 1859.

4. "Minutes, Galveston Baptist Church," 11 December 1859.

5. Ibid.

6. Ibid., 18 December 1859.

7. *Northern Standard*, 14 January 1860.

8. James Boykin to M. B. Lamar, 7 January 1840, Texas State Archives, Austin.

9. *Charleston Daily Courier*, 1 February 1860.

10. "Howard Association Minutes," 9 January 1860.

11. *The Southern Baptist*, 4 February 1860.

12. Ibid., 3 March 1860.

13. *Galveston County Deed Records*, Book L, 715.

14. *South Western Baptist*, 2 August 1860.

15. Ibid., 16 August 1860.

16. Ibid.

17. *Minutes of the 40th Anniversary of the State Convention of the Baptist Denomination in South Carolina, Held at Greenville, July 27–31, 1860* (Columbia, S.C.: *The Guardian* office, 1860), 61–65.

18. *The Southern Baptist*, 25 August 1860.

19. Ibid.

20. Ibid.

21. *Minutes of the 109th Session of the Charleston Baptist Association, Held with the High Hills Baptist Church, November 17–19, 1860* (Charleston: A. J. Burke, 1860), 10.

22. Arthur M. Wilcox and Warren Ripley, *The Civil War at Charleston* (Charleston: *The News and The Evening Press*, 1980), 2.

23. Mrs. Thomas Taylor, ed., *South Carolina Women in the Confederacy* (Columbia, S.C.: State Committee of the Daughters of the Confederacy, 1903), 170.

24. Huckins to Mary Huckins, 12 April 1861, Rosenberg Library.

25. *Proceedings of the Southern Baptist Convention at its 8th Biennial Session held in the First Baptist Church, Savannah, Ga., May 10, 11, 12, and 13, 1861* (Richmond: MacFarlane and Ferguson, Printers, 1861), 63–64.

26. Ibid.

27. *Minutes of the 41st Anniversary of the State Convention of the Baptist Denomination in South Carolina, Held at Spartanburg, July 26–28, 1861* (Columbia, S.C.: Southern Guardian Steam Power Press, 1861), 95, 132.

28. Taylor, *South Carolina Women*, 172.

29. "Minutes, Galveston Baptist Church," July 1861.

30. *Minutes of the 110th Session of the Charleston Baptist Association, Held with the Antioch Baptist Church, November 16, 1861* (Charleston: A. J. Burke, 1861), 6.

31. Ibid.

32. Ibid., 8.

33. Wilcox and Ripley, *The Civil War*, 27.

34. E. Milby Burton, *The Siege of Charleston, 1861–1865* (Columbia, S.C.: University of South Carolina Press), 80–84.

35. *Minutes of the 43rd and 44th Anniversaries of the State Convention of the Baptist Denomination in South Carolina, Held at Darlington, July 24th to 27th, 1863, and at Greenville, July 29th to August 1st, 1864* (Columbia, S.C.: F. G. DeFontaine & Co., 1864), 203.

36. James Huckins to Mary Huckins, 7 May 1862, Rosenberg Library.

37. Ibid.

38. Ibid.

39. *The Confederate Baptist*, 1 October 1862.

40. *Minutes of the 42nd Anniversary of the State Convention of the Baptist Denomination in South Carolina, Held at Greenville, July 25–28, 1862* (Columbia, S.C., 1862), 165.

41. *The Confederate Baptist*, 19 November 1862.

42. *Minutes of the 111th Session of the Charleston Baptist Association, Held with the Calvary Baptist Church, November 15–17, 1862* (Camden, S.C.: Roberts Book and Job Printers, 1864), 1–5.

43. Ibid.

44. Ibid.

45. Ibid.

Chapter 16

1. "Register of Appointments, Confederate States Army," *Index to Compiled Service Records of Confederate Soldiers* (Microfilm Box 26, Roll 234, No. 253, National Archives depositories).

2. *The Confederate Baptist*, 8 April 1863.

3. Ibid.

4. James Huckins to Brig. Gen. Thomas Jordan, Chief of Staff, Charleston, S.C., 5 August 1863. Recorded in *Index to Compiled Service Records*.

5. *Minutes of the 43rd Anniversary of the State Convention of the Baptist Denomination in South Carolina*, 203.

Cited References

BOOKS

Allen, J. M. *The United States Baptist Annual Register and Almanac.* Vol. 1. Philadelphia, 1833.

Baker, Nina Brown. *Texas Yankee, The Story of Gail Borden.* New York: Harcourt, Brace and Co., 1955.

Baker, Robert A. *Relations Between Northern and Southern Baptists.* Fort Worth, 1948.

———. *The Blossoming Desert, A Concise History of Texas Baptists.* Waco, Tex.: Word Books, 1970.

Barber, John Warner. *Historical Collections Being a General Collection of Interesting Facts, Traditions, Biographical Sketches, Anecdotes, Etc. Relating to the History and Antiquities of Every Town in Massachusetts with Geographical Descriptions.* Worcester: Warren Lazell, 1848.

———. *Massachusetts Historical Collection.* Worchester: Dorr, Howland & Co., 1839.

Buckingham, J. S. *America, Historical, Statistic and Descriptive.* Vol. 3. London: Fisher, Son and Co., 1841.

Burton, E. Milby. *The Siege of Charleston, 1861–1865.* Columbia, S.C.: University of South Carolina Press, 1970.

Carroll, J. M. *A History of Texas Baptists.* Dallas: Baptist Standard Publishing Co., 1923.

Cathcart, William. *The Baptist Encyclopedia.* Philadelphia: Louis H. Everts, 1881.

Curry, Richard O. *The Abolitionists, Reformers or Fanatics?* New York: Holt, Rinehart and Winston, 1965.

Davis, Robert E., ed. *The Diary of William Barrett Travis, August 39, 1833– June 26, 1834.* Waco: Texian Press, 1972.

Dixon, Sam Houston, and Louis Wiltz Kemp. *The Heroes of San Jacinto.* Houston: The Anson Jones Press, 1932.

Eaton, Chester W., and Warren E. Eaton, eds. *Proceedings of the 250th Anniversary of the Ancient Town of Redding [sic].* Reading, Mass.: Loring & Twombly, 1896.

Eaton, Lilly. *Genealogical History of the Town of Reading, Mass. including the present towns of Wakefield, Reading, and North Reading with Chronological and Historical Sketches, from 1639 to 1874.* Boston: Alfred Mudge & Son, Printers, 1874.

Eaton, W. H. *Historical Sketch of the Massachusetts Baptist Missionary Society and Convention, 1802–1902.* Boston: Massachusetts Baptist Convention, 1903.

Everts, Rev. N. R. *History of the First Baptist Church in Wakefield, Mass., 1800–1900.* Malden: G. E. Dunbar, 1901.

Fehrenbach, T. R. *Lone Star, A History of Texas and the Texans.* New York: Macmillan Co., 1968.

Frantz, Joe B. *Gail Borden, Dairyman to a Nation.* Norman, Okla.: University of Oklahoma Press, 1951.

Gammel, H. P. N. *The Laws of Texas.* Vol. 1. Austin: The Gammel Book Company, 1898.

Graham, Sam B., ed. *Galveston Community Book.* Galveston: Arthur H. Cawston, 1945.

Griffin, S. C. *History of Galveston.* Galveston: A. H. Cawston, 1931.

Henry, Robert Selph. *The Story of the Mexican War.* New York: The Bobbs-Merrill Company, Inc., 1950.

Kennedy, William. *Texas: The Rise, Progress and Prospects of the Republic of Texas.* Vol. 2. London: R. Hastings, 1841.

Knowlton, I. C. *Annals of Calais, Maine and St. Stephen, New Brunswick: Including the Village of Milltown, ME., and the Present town of Milltown, N.B.* Calais: J. A. Sears, Printer, 1875.

LaFayette, Wilbur. *Early History of Vermont.* Vol. 4. Jericho, Vt.: Roscoe Printing House, 1903.

Link, J. B., ed. *Texas Historical and Biographical Magazine.* Vols. 1 and 2. Austin, 1891.

Mallary, C. D. *Memoirs of Elder Jesse Mercer.* New York: Lewis Colby, 1844.

Meller, Grenville, ed. *A Book of the United States Exhibiting its Geography, Divisions, Constitution and Government.* Hartford: H. F. Sumner & Co., 1838.

Morrell, Z. N. *Flowers and Fruits from the Wilderness, or Thirty-Six Years in Texas and Two Winters in Honduras.* 1872. Reprint. Waco, Tex.: The Markham Press Fund of Baylor University Press, 1976.

Murray, Lois Smith. *Baylor At Independence.* Waco, Tex.: Baylor University Press, 1972.

Nance, Joseph Milton. *Attack and Counter-Attack, The Texas-Mexican Frontier, 1842.* Austin: University of Texas Press, 1964.

Putnam, Mary Burnham. *The Baptists and Slavery, 1840–1845.* Ann Arbor, Mich.: George Wahr, 1913.

Hansell, George H. *Reminiscences of Baptist Churches and Baptist Leaders in New York City and Vicinity, From 1835–1898.* New York: American Baptist Publication Society, 1899.

Hayes, Charles W. *History of the Island and the City of Galveston.* Cincinnati, 1879.

Haynes, Harry. *The Life and Writings of Rufus C. Burleson.* Compiled and Published by Mrs. Georgia J. Burleson, 1901.

Hooton, Charles. *St. Louis Isle or Texiana with Additional Observations Made in the United States and in Canada.* London: Simmons and Ward, 1847.

Richardson, W. & D. *Galveston Directory for 1859–60: With a Brief History of the Island Prior to the Foundation of the City.* Galveston: *News* Book and Job Office, 1859.

Sprague, William B. *Annals of the American Pulpit or Commemorative Notices of Distinguished American Clergymen of Various Denominations.* New York: Robert Carter & Brothers, 1860.

Taylor, Mrs. Thomas, ed. *South Carolina Women in the Confederacy.* Columbia, S.C.: State Committee of the Daughters of the Confederacy, 1903.

Webb, Walter Prescott, ed. *The Handbook of Texas.* Vols. 1 and 2. Austin: The Texas State Historical Association, 1952.

Wilcox, Arthur M., and Warren Ripley. *The Civil War at Charleston.* Charleston: The News and The Evening Press, 1980.

Williams, Mrs. Catherine B. *Biography of Revolutionary Heroes: Containing the Life of Brigadier Gen. William Barton, and also, of Captain Stephen Olney.* Providence: Published by the Author, 1839.

NEWSPAPERS

The Baptist Advocate (New York), 6 July 1839, 7 December 1839, 2 February 1840.

Baptist Banner and Western Pioneer (Louisville, Ky.), 30 June 1842, 18 August 1842.

Charleston Courier (Charleston, S.C.), 12 November 1859.

The Christian Index (Penfield, Ga.), 7 February 1839, 14 March 1839, 12 December 1839, 14 May 1840, 1 October 1840, 8 October 1840, 15 October 1840, 28 May 1841, 21 January 1842, 15 April 1842, 28 April 1843, 19 August 1847, 25 December 1920.

The Civilian and Galveston Gazette (Galveston, Tex.), 20 November 1847.

The Confederate Baptist (Columbia, S.C.), 1 October 1862, 19 November 1862, 26 November 1862, 25 March 1863, 8 April 1863, 2 September 1863.

Northern Standard (Clarksville, Tex.), 14 January 1860.

The Southern Baptist (Charleston, S.C.), 31 May 1859, 3 March 1860, 25 August 1860.

South Western Baptist (Marion, Ala.), 6 January 1852, 18 February 1852, 9 April 1857, 2 August 1860, 16 August 1860.

South Western Baptist Chronicle (New Orleans), 27 November 1847.

The Texas Baptist (Anderson, Tex.), 14 November 1855.

Texas Telegraph and Register (Houston), 29 May 1839.

LETTERS

(Location of original or photocopies of letters indicated in Notes.)

Baylor, R. E. B., to: James Huckins, 1 March 1859; J. H. Stribling, 13 April 1871.

Borden, Gail, Jr., to: Executive Committee, American Baptist Home Mission Society, 5 March 1843, 25 March 1845; Reverend Basil Manly, 2 July 1845, 22 March 1846.

Cole, J. P., to: Gail Borden, Jr., 11 March, 1855, 15 April 1855, 18 May 1855.

Fellows, George, to: Bro. Sawyer, October 1844.

The First Baptist Church of Galveston, to: Union Baptist Association, [1853].

Furman, H. H., to: Judge B. C. Franklin, 21 January 1840.

Huckins, James, to: J. P. Cole, 23 June 1853; S. H. Cone (In *The Baptist Advocate,* 27 June 1840); Mary Huckins, 12 April 1861, 7 May 6 1862; Rhoda Barton Huckins, 29 December 1838, 11 July 1846, 18 July 1846.

Huckins, Rhoda Barton, to: her sister, Emeline, 8 September 1840.

Malthy, Mary Wharton, to: General Carvajal, n.d.

Stevenson, J. R., to: Eugene W. Baker, 21 July 1983.

Trask, Francis, to: Israel Trask, 5 July 1835.

MINUTES AND PROCEEDINGS

American Baptist Home Mission Society, New York:

The Seventh Report of the Executive Committee of the American Baptist Home Mission Society, Presented at its Anniversary in Philadelphia, April 16, 1839, with the Treasurer's Report. New York: Mission Rooms, 1839.

The Eighth Report of the American Baptist Home Mission Society, Presented by the Executive Committee at the Anniversary in New York, April 28, 1840 with the Treasurer's Report. New York: Mission Rooms, 1840.

The Ninth Report of the American Baptist Home Mission Society presented by the Executive Committee at the Anniversary in Baltimore, April 27, 1841. New York: Mission Rooms, 1841.

The Eleventh Report of the American Baptist Home Mission Society presented by the Executive Committee at the Anniversary in Albany, N.Y., April 25, 1843. New York: Mission Rooms, 1843.

Thirteenth Report of the American Baptist Home Mission Society presented by the Executive Board at the Anniversary at Providence, Rhode Island, April 29, 1845. New York: Baptist Home Mission Rooms, 1845.

Georgia:

Minutes of the 15th Anniversary of the Georgia Baptist Convention, Held at Talbottom, Georgia on the 29th & 30th April and 2nd & 3rd of May, 1836. N.p., n.d.

Eighteenth Anniversary of the Georgia Baptist Convention, Held at Richland, Twiggs County, Geo. On the 3d, 4th & 6th days of May, 1839. Washington: Printed by M. J. Kappel at the Office of *The Christian Index*, 1839.

Maine:

Minutes of the Maine Baptist Convention, 12th Anniversary, Holden in Bangor, October 5th and 6th, 1836. Charles Day and Co., Printers, 1836.

Minutes of the Maine Baptist Convention, Held at Waterville, October 3 & 4, 1838. Brunswick: T. W. Newman, Printers, 1838.

Massachusetts:

Minutes, Boston Baptist Association, Held at the First Baptist Meeting House in Charlestown on Wednesday and Thursday, September 19 & 20, 1827, being its Sixteenth Anniversary. Boston: Lincoln & Edmands, Printers, 1827.

Minutes of the Fiftieth Session of the Salem Baptist Association Held with the First Baptist Church in Beverly, October 10 and 11, 1877. Boston: J. M. Hewes, 1877.

New Hampshire:

Minutes of the Woodstock Association, Held at Newport, New Hampshire, September 27–28, 1826. Simeon Ide., 1825.

Southern Baptist Convention:

Proceedings of the First Triennial Meeting of the Southern Baptist Convention, Held at Richmond, Virginia, June 10, 11, 12, 13, and 15, 1846. Richmond: H. K. Ellyson, 1846.

Proceedings of the Southern Baptist Convention at its 8th Biennial Session held in the First Baptist Church, Savannah, Ga., May 10, 11, 12, and 13, 1861. Richmond: MacFarlane and Ferguson, Printers, 1861.

South Carolina:

Minutes of the 108th Session of the Charleston Baptist Association held with the Congaree Baptist Church, November 19–22, 1859. Charleston, 1860.

Minutes of the 109th Session of the Charleston Baptist Association, Held with the High Hills Baptist Church, November 17–19, 1860. Charleston: A. J. Burke, 1860.

Minutes of the 110th Session of the Charleston Baptist Association, Held with the Antioch Baptist Church, November 16, 1861. Charleston: A. J. Burke, 1861.

Minutes of the 111th Session of the Charleston Baptist Association, Held with the Calvary Baptist Church, November 15–17, 1862. Camden, S.C.: Roberts Book and Job Printers, 1864.

Minutes of the State Convention of the Baptist Denomination in South Carolina at its 19th Anniversary, Held at the Black Swamp Church, Beaufort District, December 7th and continued to December 10th, 1839. N.p., n.d.

Minutes of the 40th Anniversary of the State Convention of the Baptist Denomination in South Carolina, Held at Greenville, July 27–31, 1860. Columbia, S.C.: *Guardian* Office, 1860.

Minutes of the 41st Anniversary of the State Convention of the Baptist Denomination in South Carolina, Held at Spartanburg, July 26–28, 1861. Columbia, S.C.: *Southern Guardian* Steam Power Press, 1861.

Minutes of the 42nd Anniversary of the State Convention of the Baptist Denomination in South Carolina, Held at Greenville, July 25–28, 1862, Columbia, S.C.: *Southern Guardian* office, 1862.

Minutes of the 43rd and 44th Anniversaries of the State Convention of the Baptist Denomination in South Carolina, Held at Darlington, July 24th to 27th, 1863 and at Greenville, July 29 to Aug. 1, 1864. Columbia, S.C., 1864.

Texas:

Organization and Proceedings of the Baptist State Convention of Texas, Held with the Antioch Church, Anderson, Grimes County, September 8—12. Huntsville: Banner Print, 1948.

Proceedings of the First Anniversary of the Baptist State Convention of Texas, Held in the city of Houston, May 11—14, 1849. Huntsville: Office of the *Texas Banner*, 1849.

Minutes of the Fifth Annual Session of the Baptist State Convention of Texas, Held at Marshall, in June, 1852. Washington; *Lone Star* Office, 1852.

Minutes of the Seventh Annual Session of the Baptist State Convention, of Texas, Held at Palestine, Anderson County, In June, 1854. Anderson, Tex.: *Central Texian* Office, 1854.

Minutes of the Eighth Annual Session of the Baptist State Convention of the State of Texas, Held at Independence, Washington County, in November, 1855. Anderson, Tex.: *Texas Baptist* Office, 1855.

Proceedings of the Baptist State Convention Held with the Church in Anderson on Saturday Before the Fourth Sabbath in October, 1856. Anderson, Tex.: Office of *The Texas Baptist*, 1856.

Proceedings of the Baptist State Convention held with the Huntsville Baptist Church, Commencing on Saturday, October 24, 1857. Anderson, Tex.: The *Texas Baptist* Offices, 1857.

Minutes of the FIrst Session of the Union Baptist Association Begun and Held in the Town of Travis in Western Texas, Oct. 8th, 1840. Houston: Telegraph Press, 1840, Reprint.

Minutes of the Second Annual Session of the Union Baptist Association held at the Clear Creek Meeting House Near Rutersville in Western Texas, Commencing on the 7th October, A.D. 1841. N.p., n.d.

Minutes of the Fourth Anniversary Meeting of the Union Baptist Association convened at Providence Church, Washington County, October 6, 1843 and Days Following. Washington: Thomas Johnson, Printers, 1843.

Minutes of the Seventh Annual Meeting of the Union Baptist Association Held with the Dove Church, Caldwell, Burleson County, on the 1st day of October, 1846 and days following. N.p., n.d.

Minutes of the Eighth Annual Meeting of the Union Baptist Association Held with the First Baptist Church in Houston, Texas Commencing on Thursday, September 20 and Ending October 4, 1847. N.p., n.d.

Minutes of the Ninth Anniversary of the Union Baptist Association Held with the Independence Church, Washington Co., Texas Commencing Sept. 28, and ending Oct. 2, 1848. N.p., n.d.

Minutes of the Sixteenth Annual Meeting of the Union Baptist Association Held with New Year's Creek Church, at Brenham, Washington County, Texas, Commencing Oct. 5, and closing Oct. 8, 1855. Galveston: Civilian Book and Job Office, 1855.

Minutes of the 17th Annual Session of the Union Baptist Association held with Laurel Hill Church at Cold Spring, Polk County, Texas, Commencing October 3d and Closing October 6th, 1856. Anderson, Tex.: Office of the *Texas Baptist*, 1856.

Minutes of the 18th Annual Session of the Union Baptist Association held with Bethany Church, Grimes County, Texas. Anderson, Tex.: Office of the *Texas Baptist*, 1857.

UNPUBLISHED MINUTES AND PROCEEDINGS

"Records of the First Baptist Church in Houston," Houston, Texas.

"Minutes, Wetumpka Baptist Church," Wetumpka, Alabama, 1839-1840.

"Minutes, Good Hope Baptist Church," Talledega, Alabama, 1836-1839.

"Minutes, Eufaula Baptist Church," Eufaula, Alabama, 1837-1840.

"Minutes of the First Baptist Church," Andover, Massachusetts, 1832-1835.

"Minutes, Galveston Baptist Church," Galveston, Texas, 1840-1865.

"Baylor University Board of Trustee Minutes," Independence, Texas, 1845-1886.

"Howard Association of Galveston, 1854-1882," Galveston, Texas.

JOURNALS AND ARTICLES

Grusendorf, Arthur A. "A Century of Education in Washington County, Texas." Revised from unpublished Ph.D. dissertation, "The Social and Philosophical Determinants of Education in Washington County since 1835." University of Texas, Austin, 1938.

Hildreth, Peggy. "The Howard Association of Galveston: The 1850s, Their Peak Years," *East Texas Historical Journal* 17, no. 2 (1979): 33–43.

Hardon, Henry Winthrop. "Huckins Family, A Reprint with Corrections and Considerable Additions." In *The New England Historical and Genealogical Register, 1913–1915*. Privately Printed, 1916.

The Southern Baptist Missionary Journal (Published in Richmond by Boards of Foreign and Domestic Missions of the Southern Baptist Convention) Vol. 1, no. 6 (November 1846); Vol. 2, no. 2 (July 1847); Vol. 2, no. 3 (August 1847); Vol. 2, no. 4 (September 1847); Vol. 2, no. 8 (January 1848); Vol. 2, no. 10 (March 1848); Vol. 3, no. 4 (September 1848); Vol. 3, no. 11 (April 1849); Vol. 4, no. 1 (June 1849); Vol. 4, no. 4 (September 1849).

MISCELLANEOUS

Baylor University Charter

Catalogue of the Members of the Literary Adelphi of the Academical and Theological Institution at New Hampton, New Hampshire. Concord: Morrill, Silsby and Co., 1844.

Catalogue of the Officers and Students of the Academic and Theological Institution, New Hampton, N.H. Concord: R. H. Sherburne & Co., 1829.

Document, Commonwealth of Massachusetts. 28 February 1835. Andover, Mass.

Galveston County Deed Records. Book L. Galveston, Tex.

General Catalogue [Colgate University]. Vol. 1. Hamilton, N.Y., 1937.

Historical Sketch of the New Hampton Institution, New Hampton, N.H. Bristol, N.H.: R. W. Musgrove, 1876.

"James Huckins," registrar materials, Brown University, Providence, R.I.

List of the Members of the First Baptist Church in Providence with Biographical Sketches of the Pastors. Providence: H. H. Brown, 1832.

"Passenger Lists, Port of Galveston, December 30, 1840." Austin, Tex.: State Archives.

"Register of Appointments, Confederate States Army." *Index to Compiled Service Records of Confederate Soldiers,* Microfilm Box 26, Roll 234, No. 253, National Archives depositories.

"Republic of Texas, County Jasper, Town Zavala, May 10, 1836." Austin, Tex.: Government Land Office.

Rules and By-Laws of the Wentworth Street Baptist Church. Charleston, S.C.: Waker, Evans and Co., 1859.

Triennial Catalogue of the Library and the Members of the Philermenian Society in Brown University. Founded A.D. 1795. Providence, R.I., *1849.*

CPSIA information can be obtained at www.ICGtesting.com
Printed in the USA
BVOW020619050412

286926BV00001B/8/P